I0483295

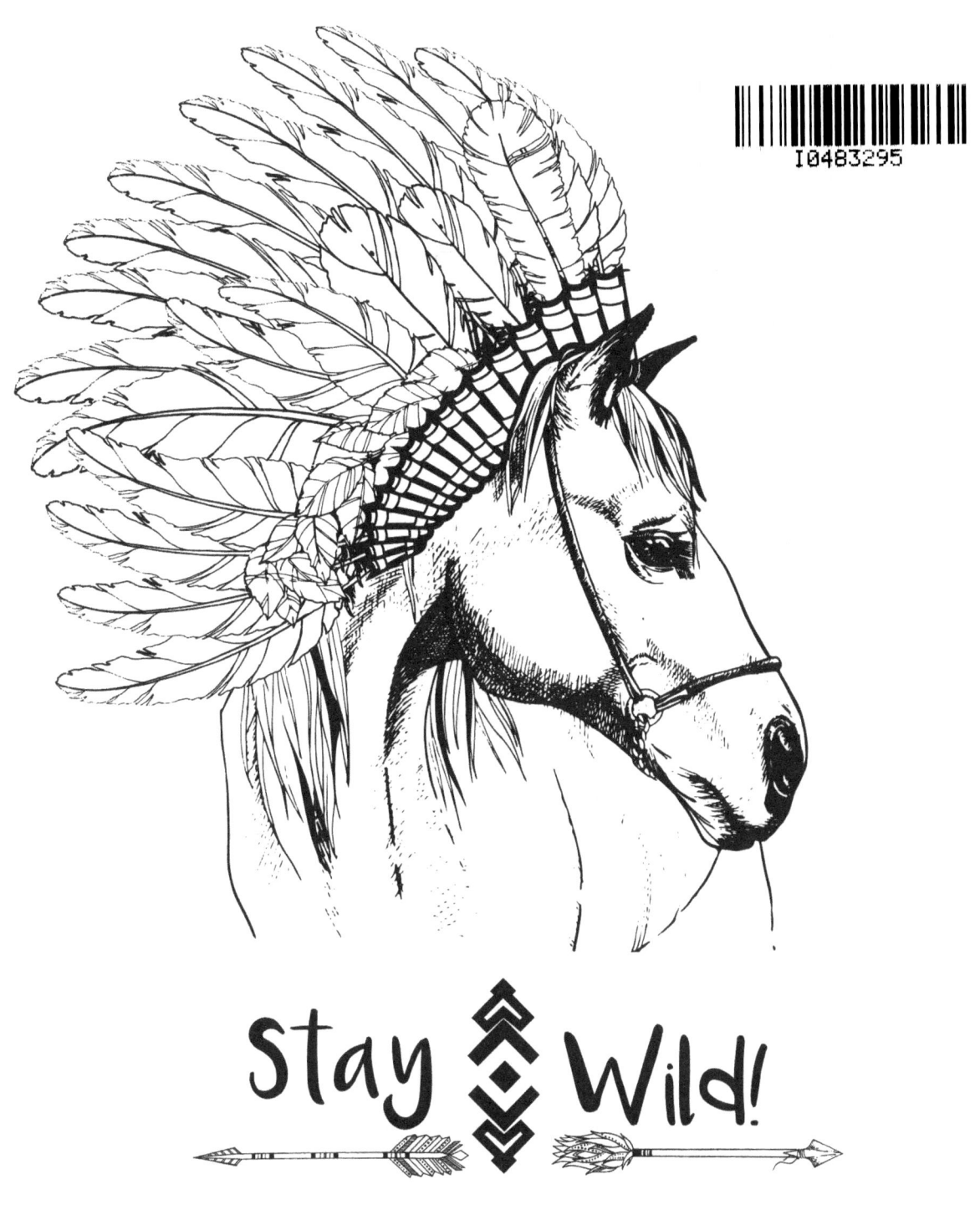

Stay ♦ Wild!

COLORING BOOK
FOR ADULTS
NATIVE AMERICAN INSPIRED

▲ ART THERAPY COLORING

Preview of Coloring Pages

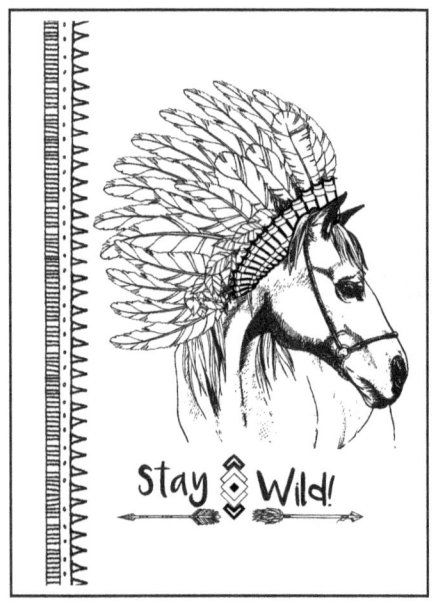

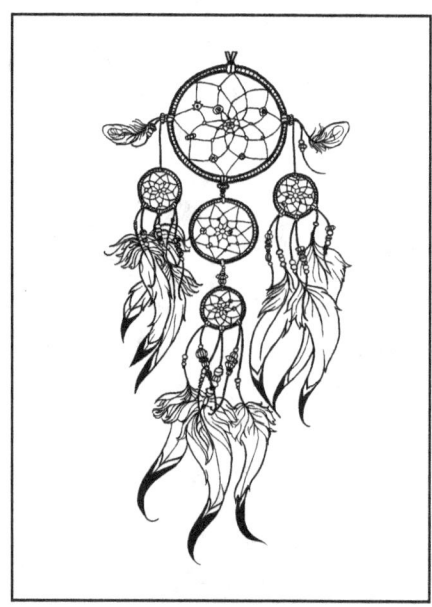

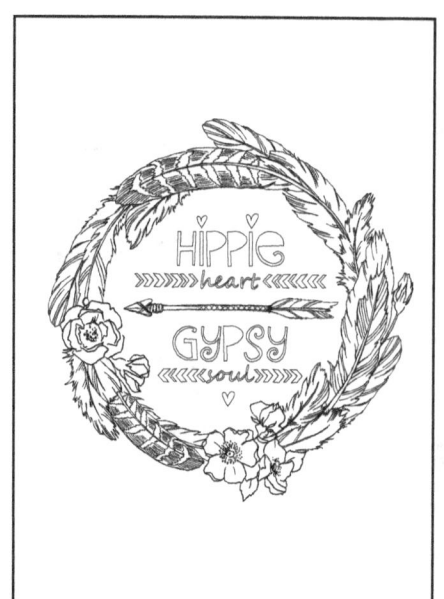

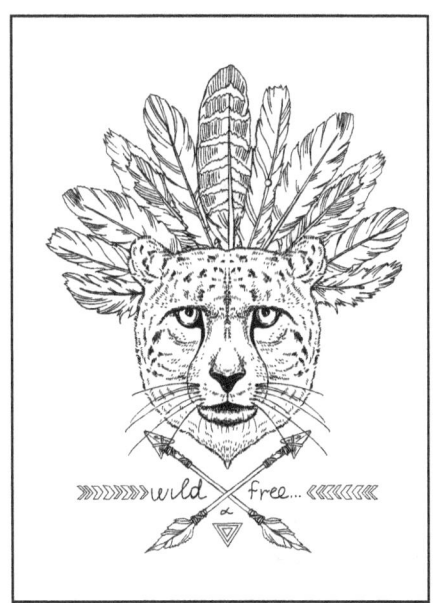

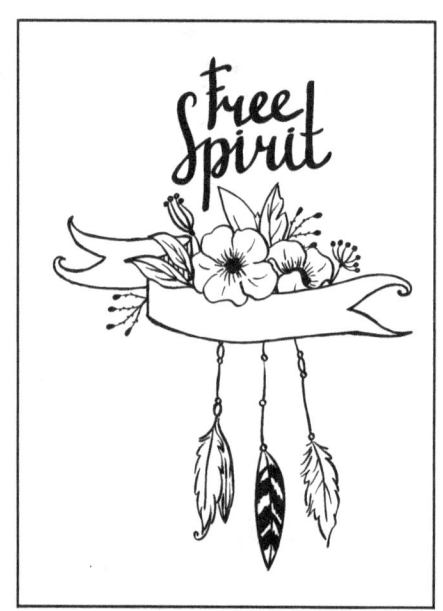

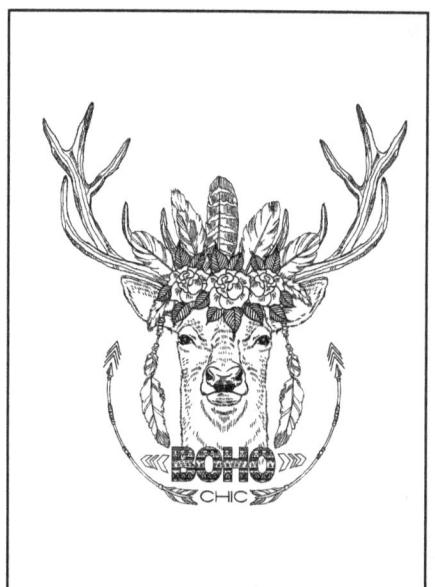

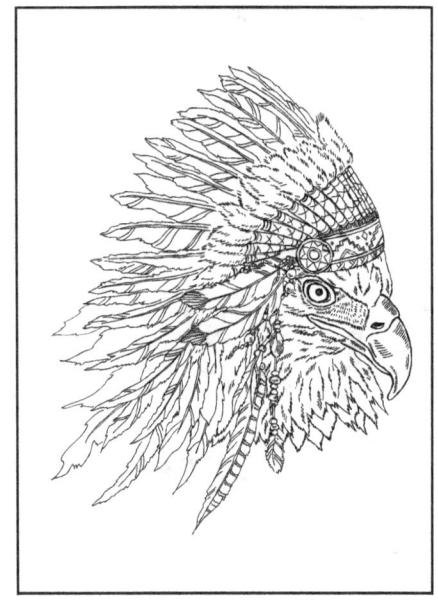

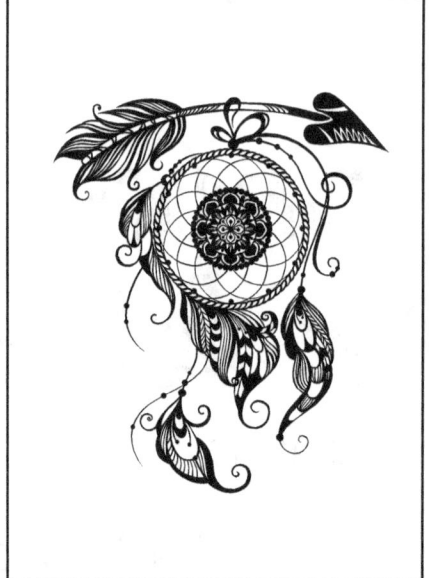

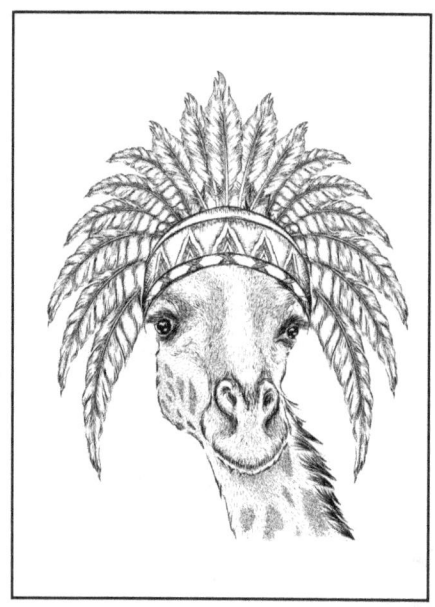

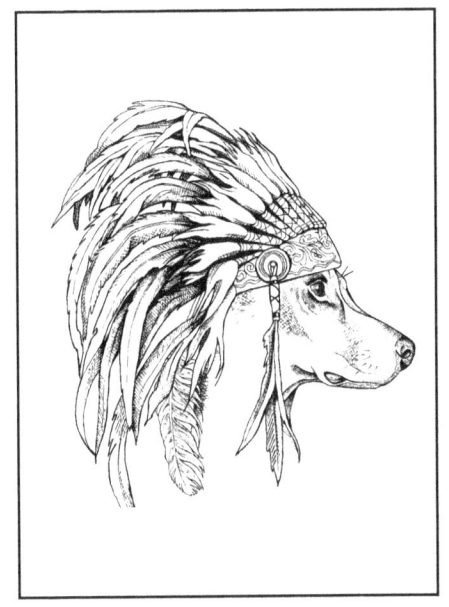

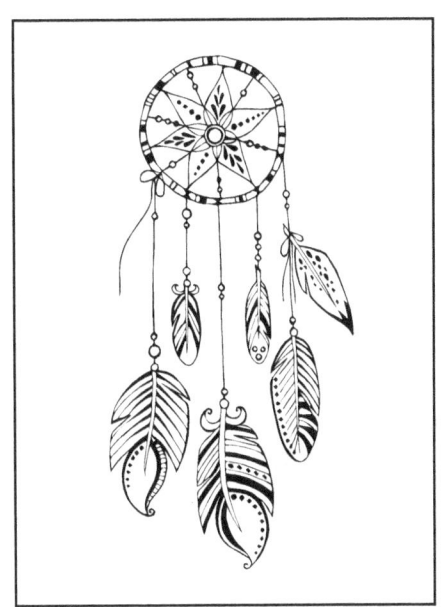

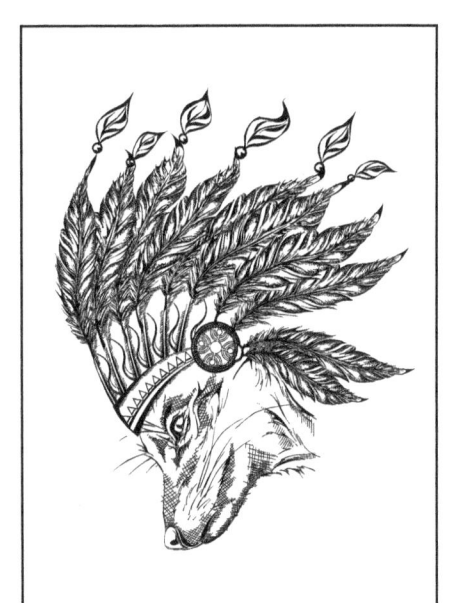

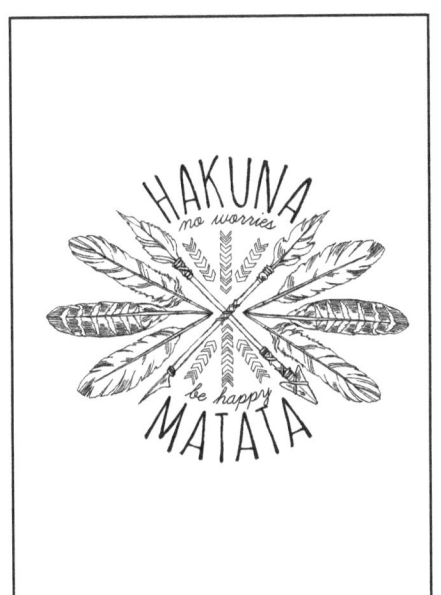

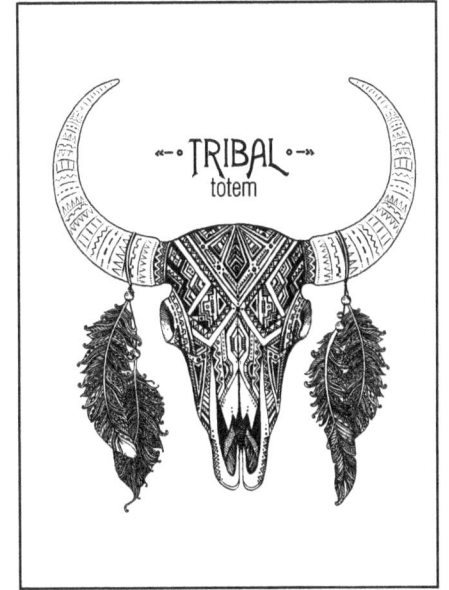

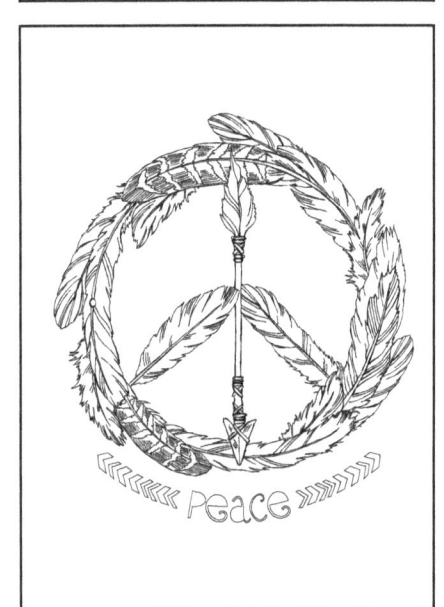

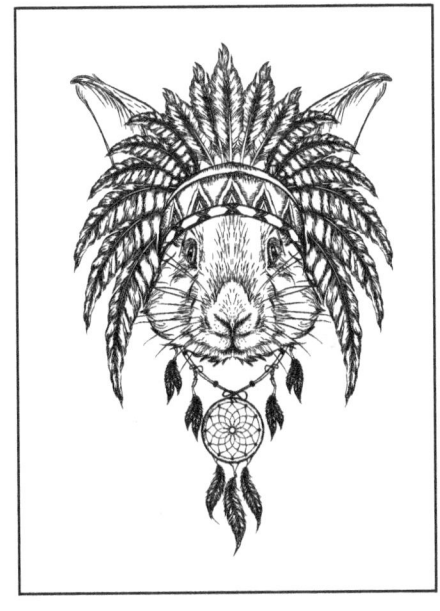

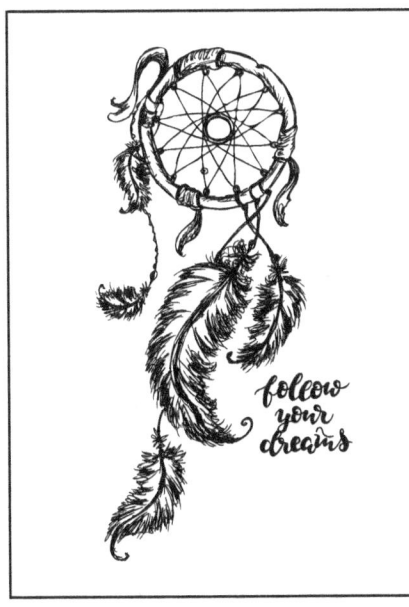

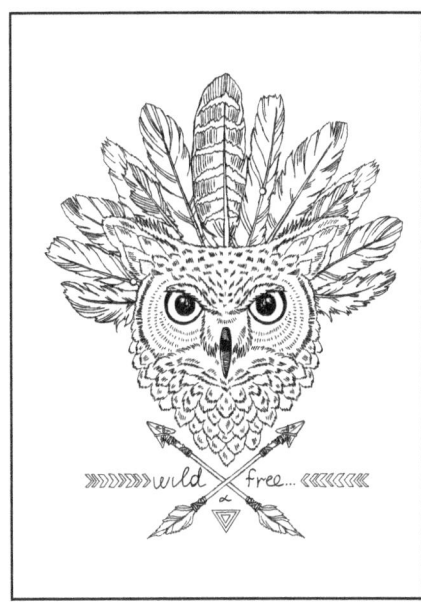

Preview of Coloring Pages

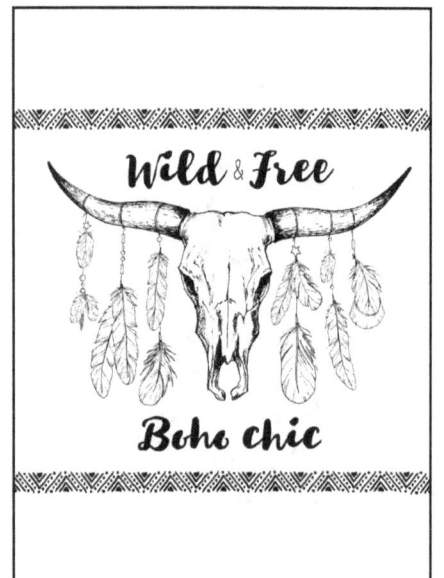
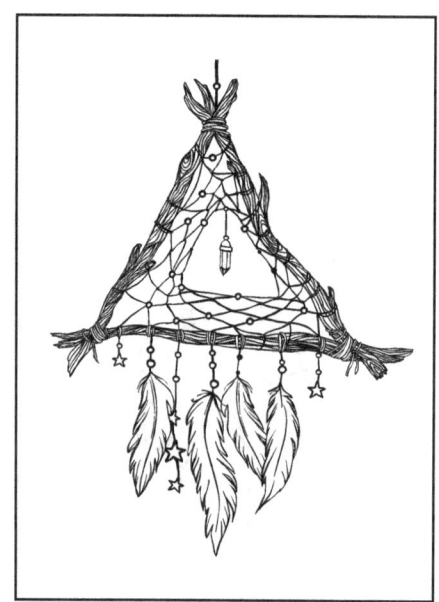
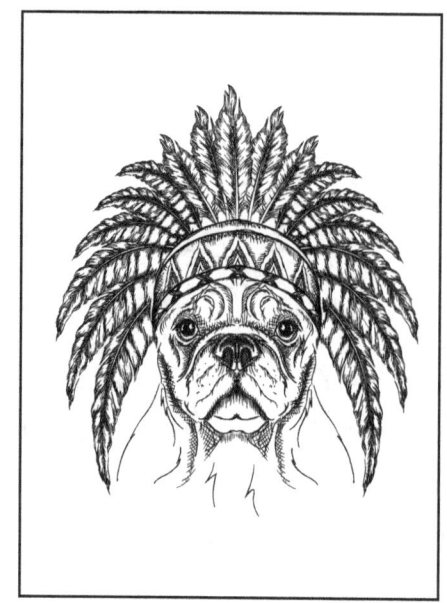
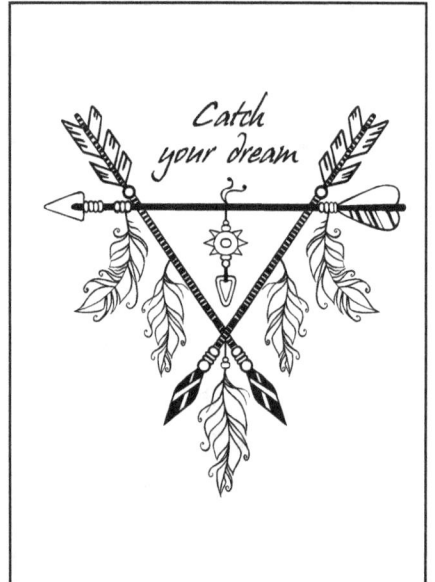
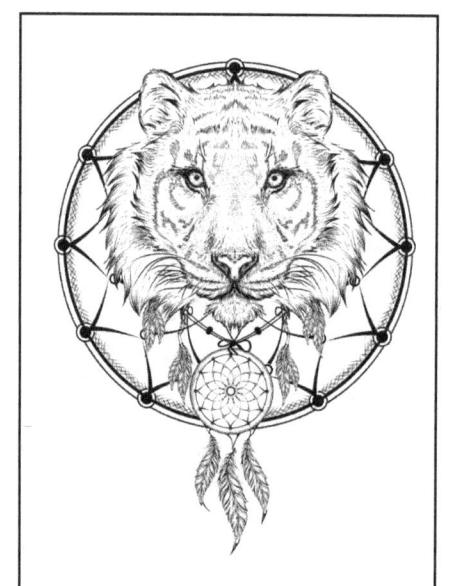
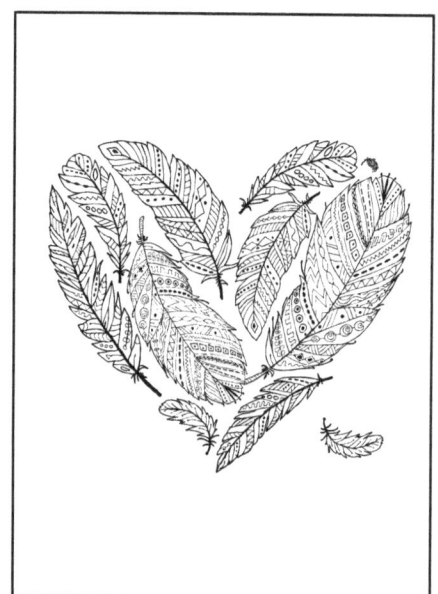
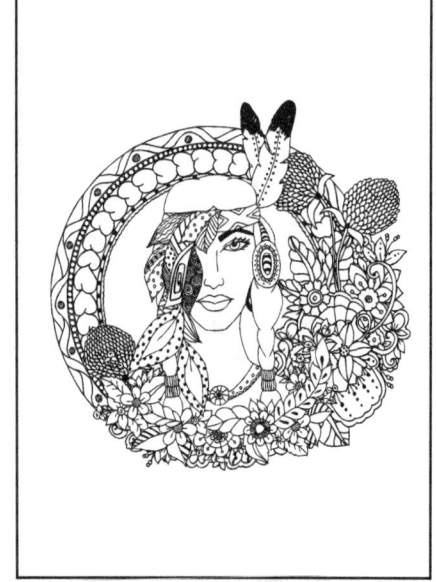
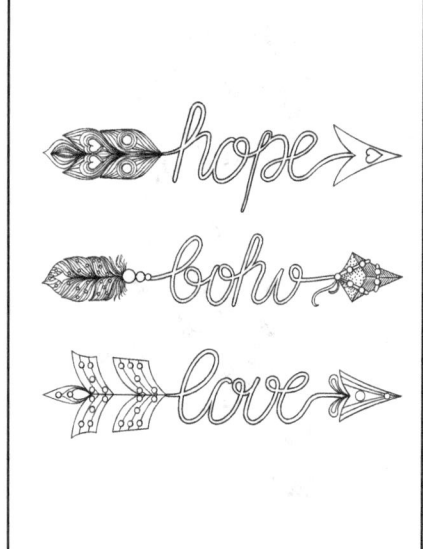
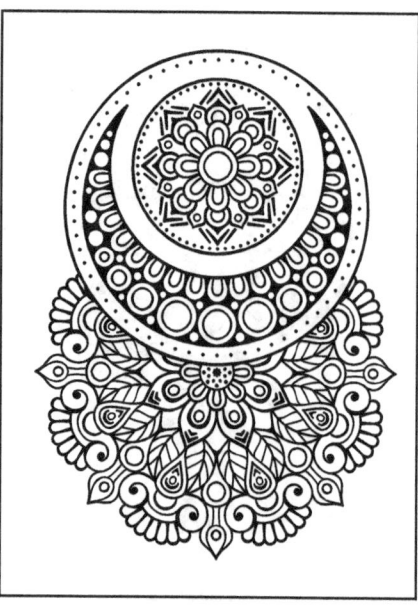

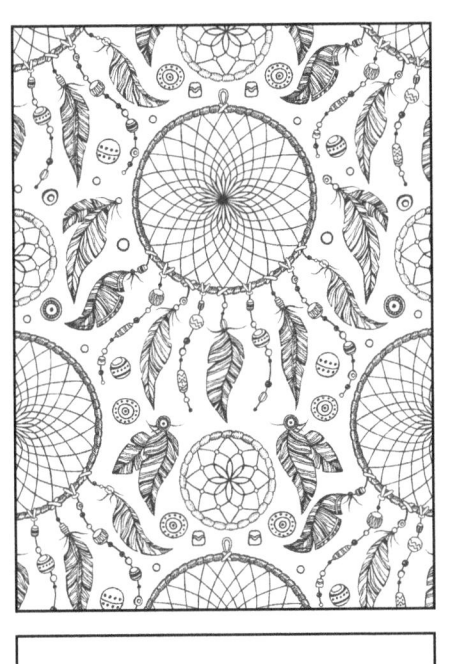
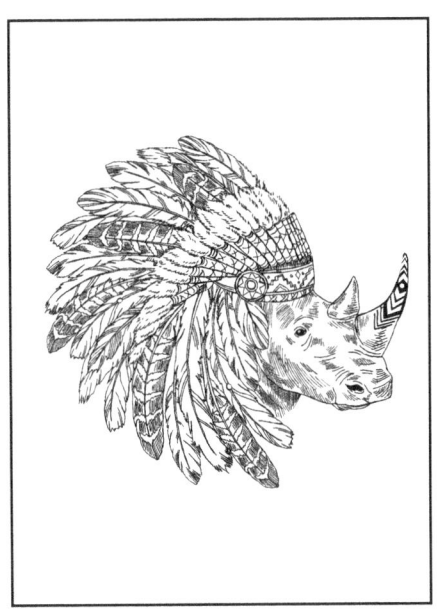
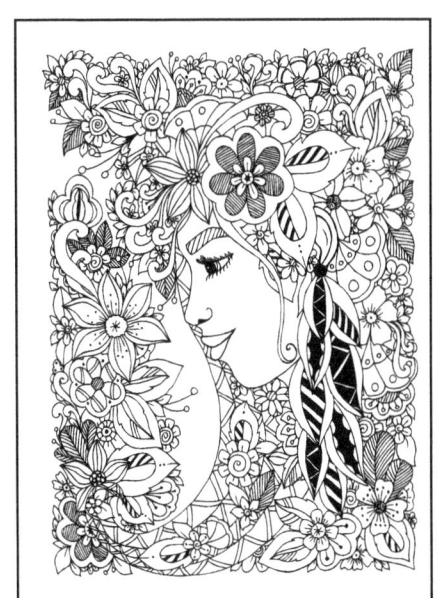
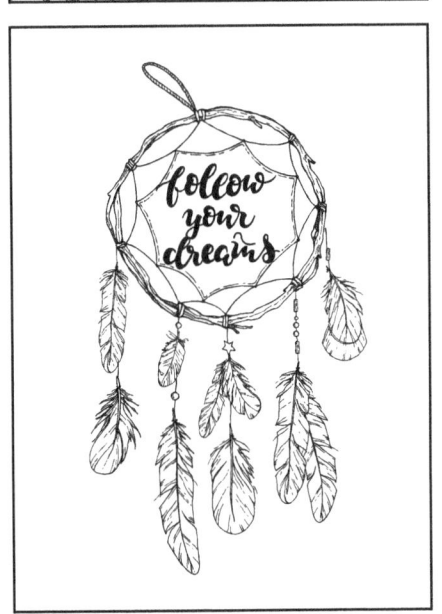
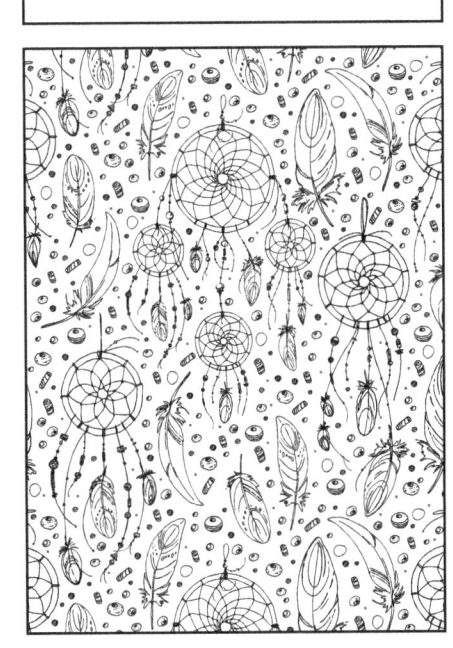
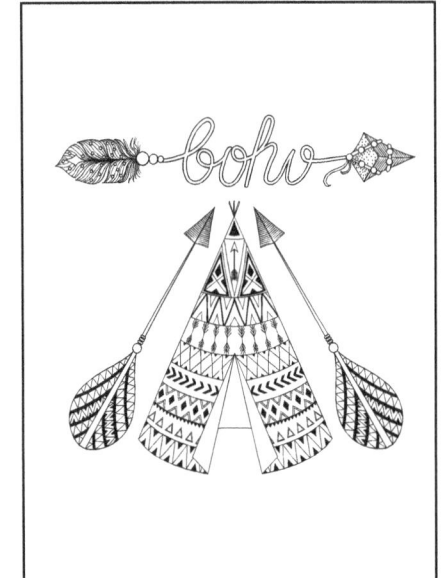
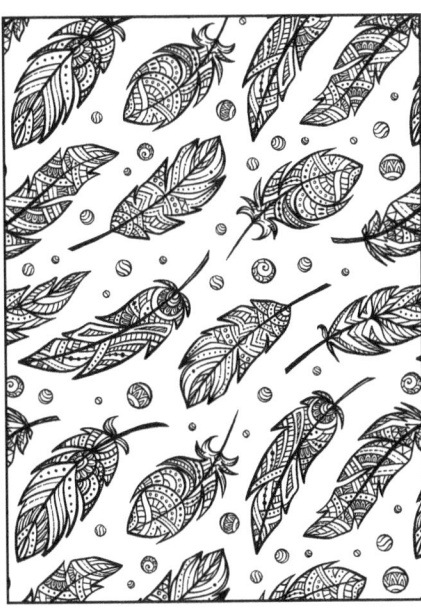
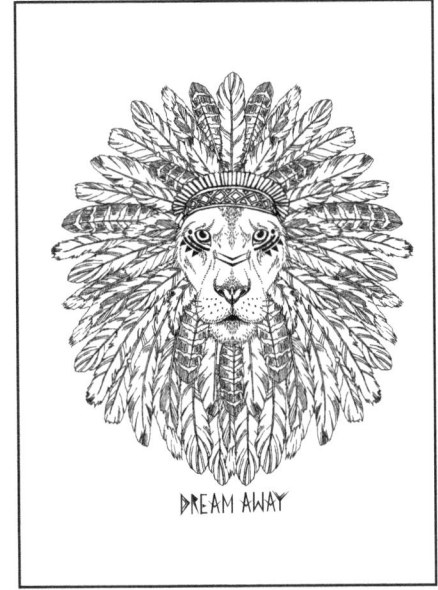
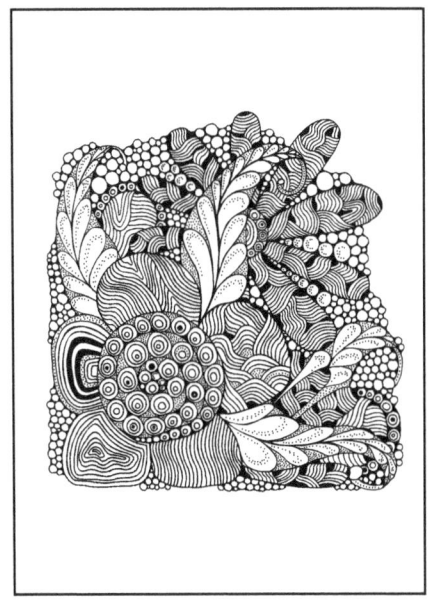

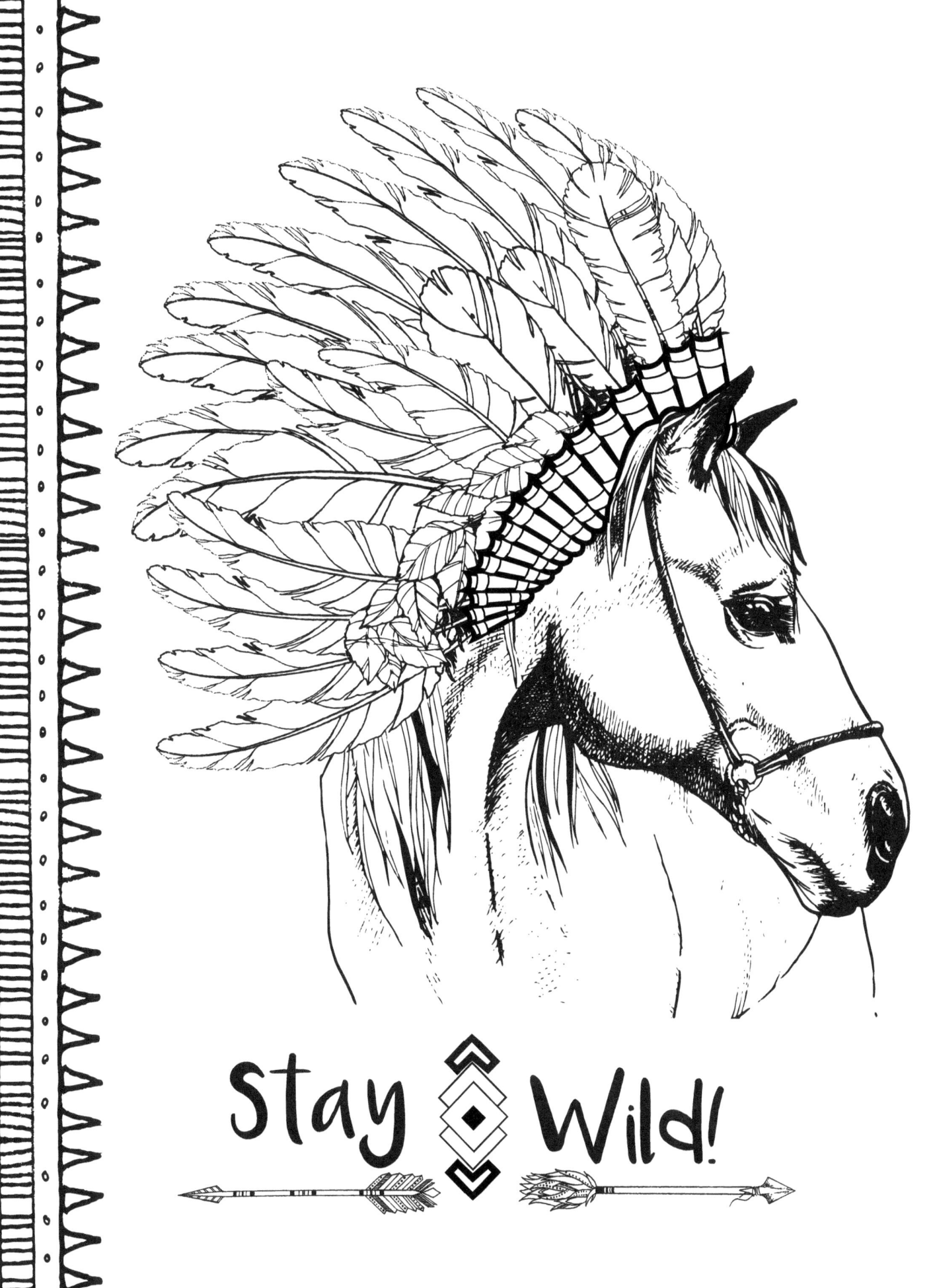

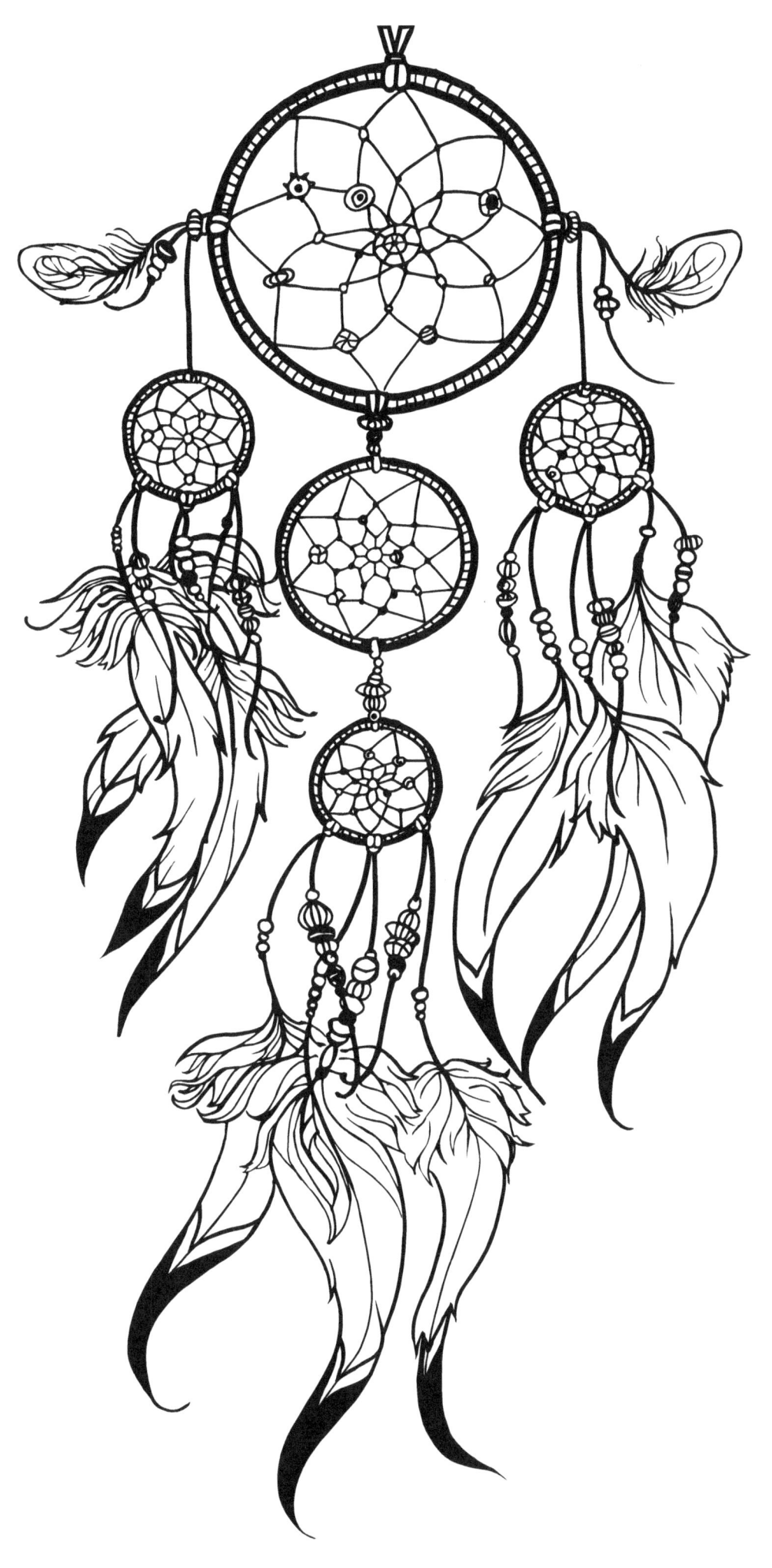

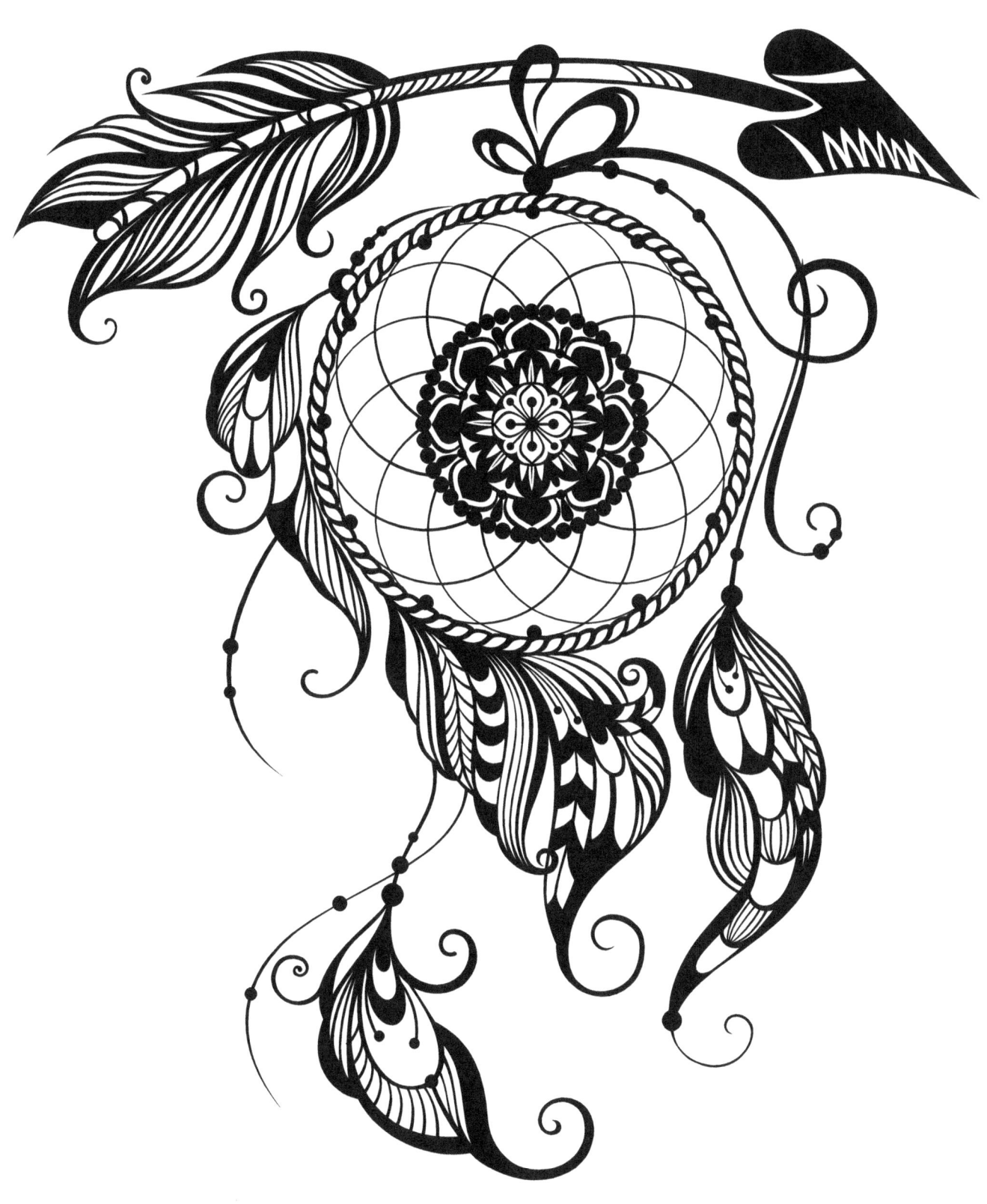

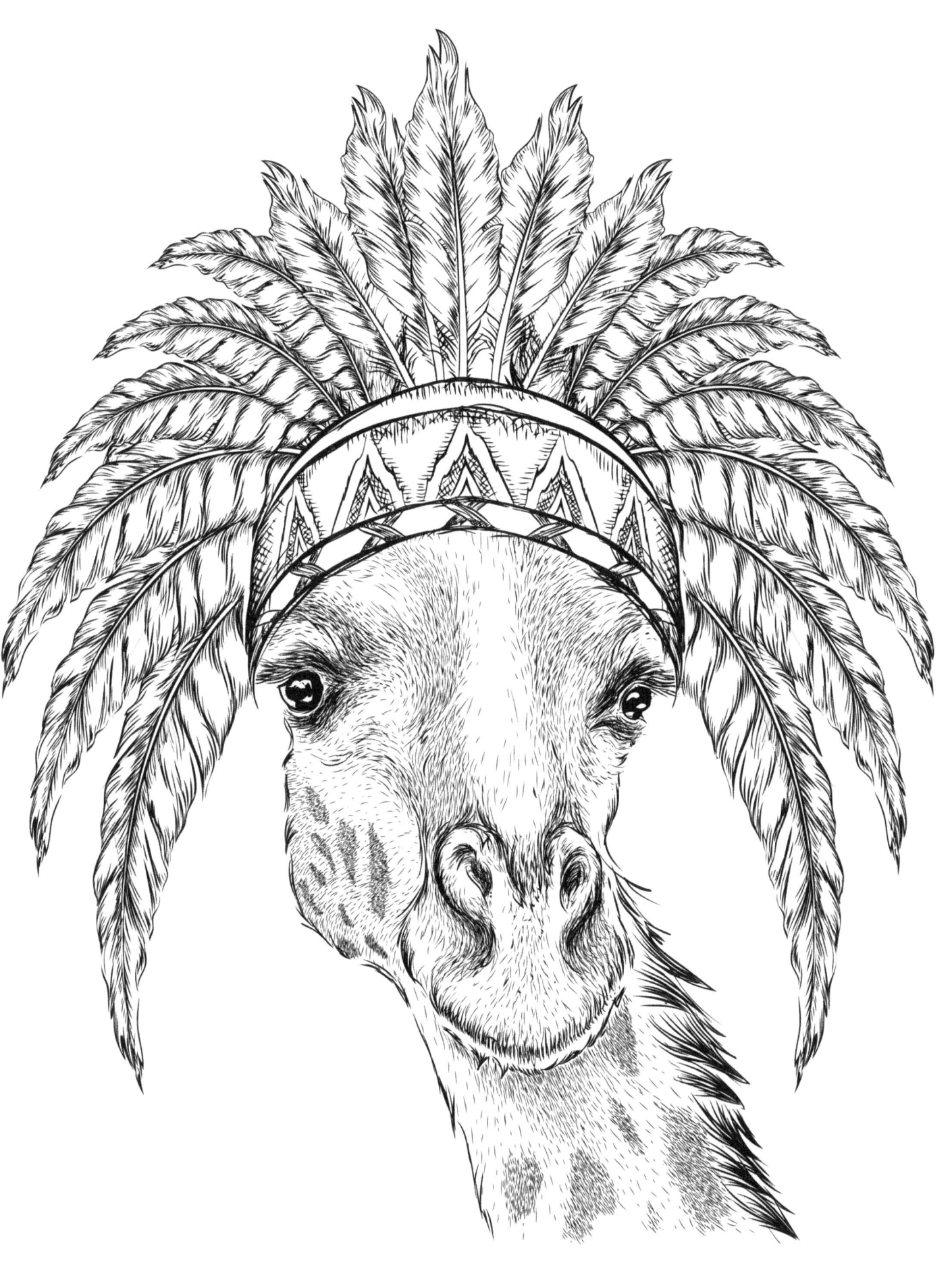

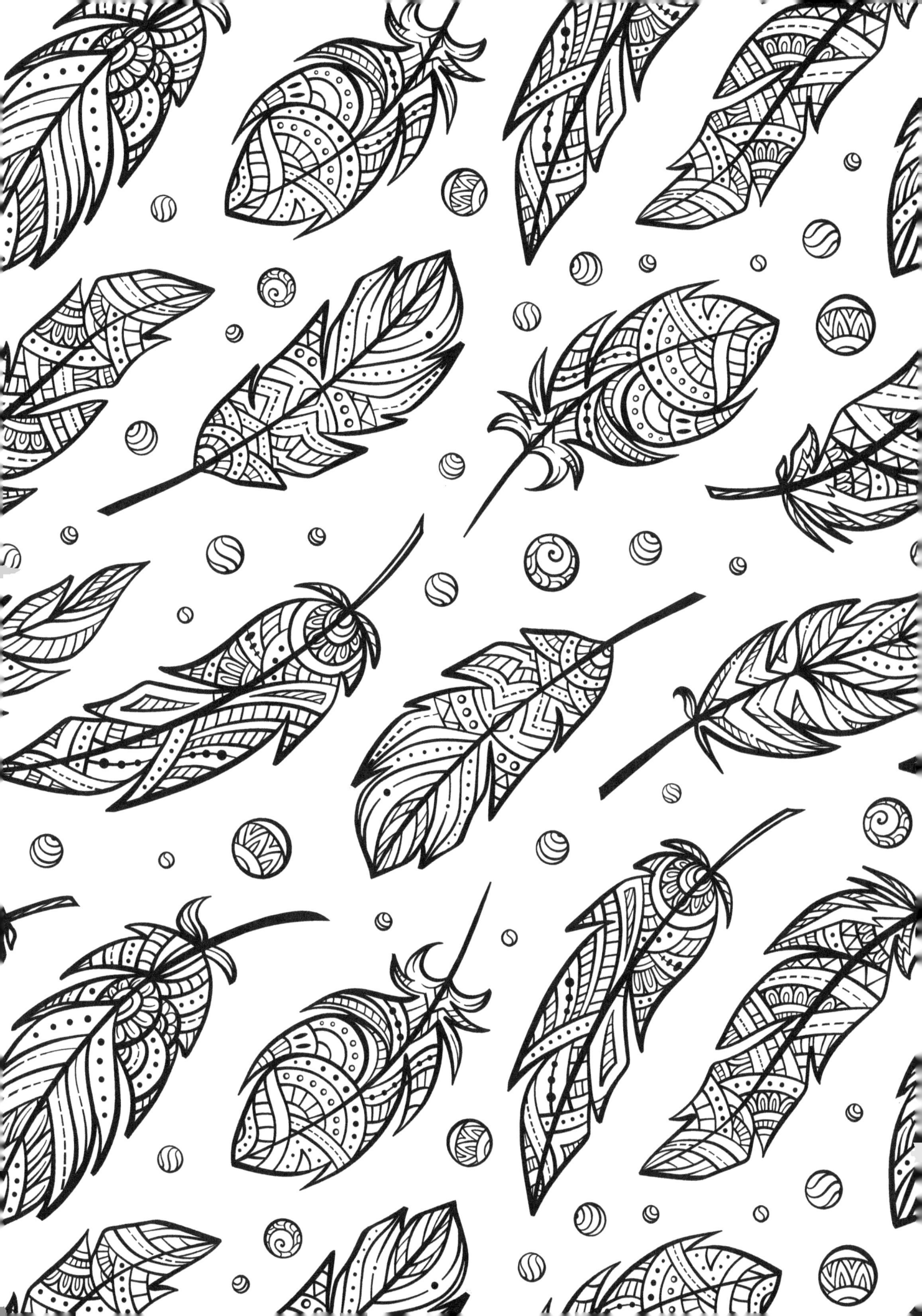

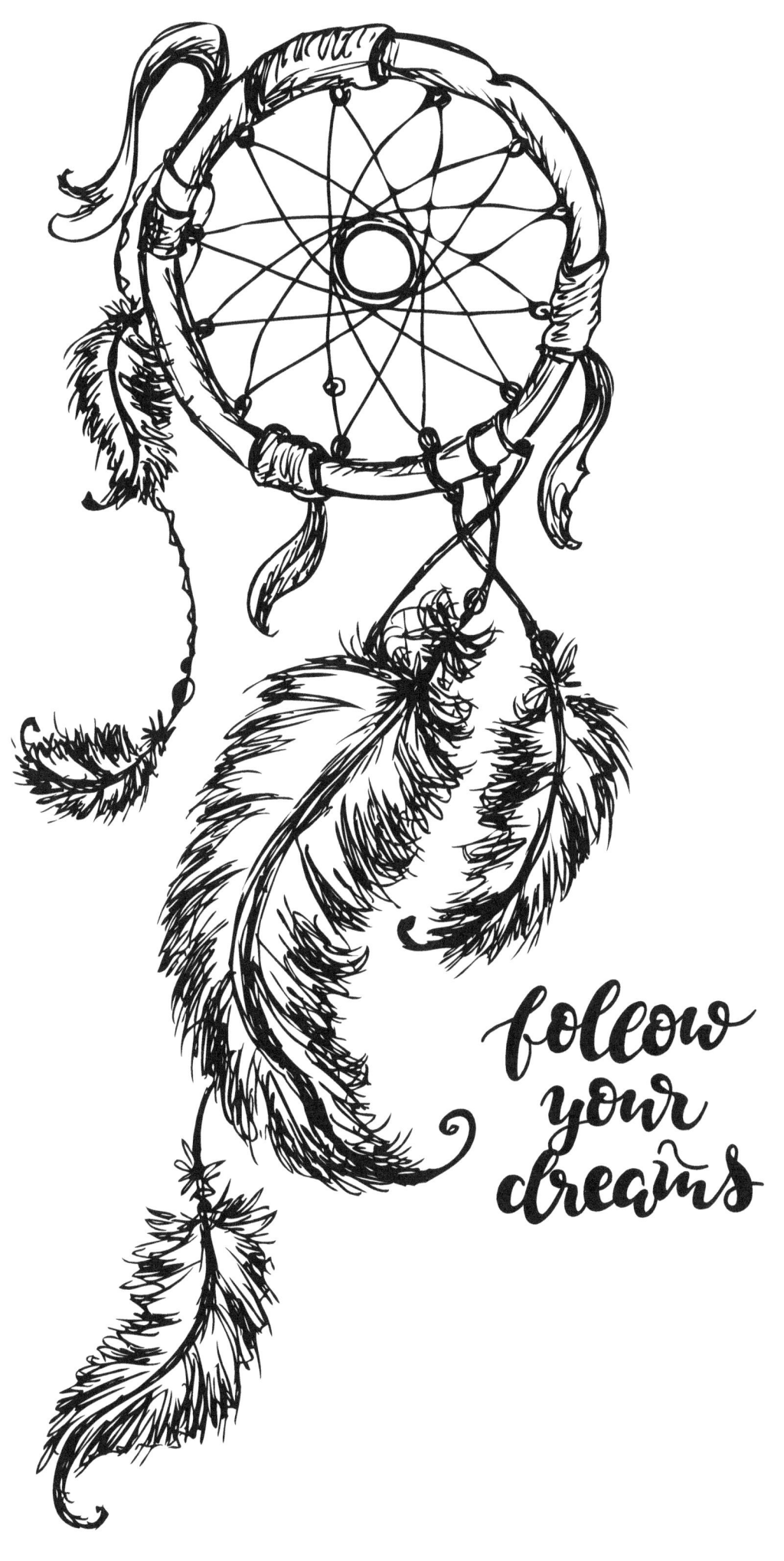

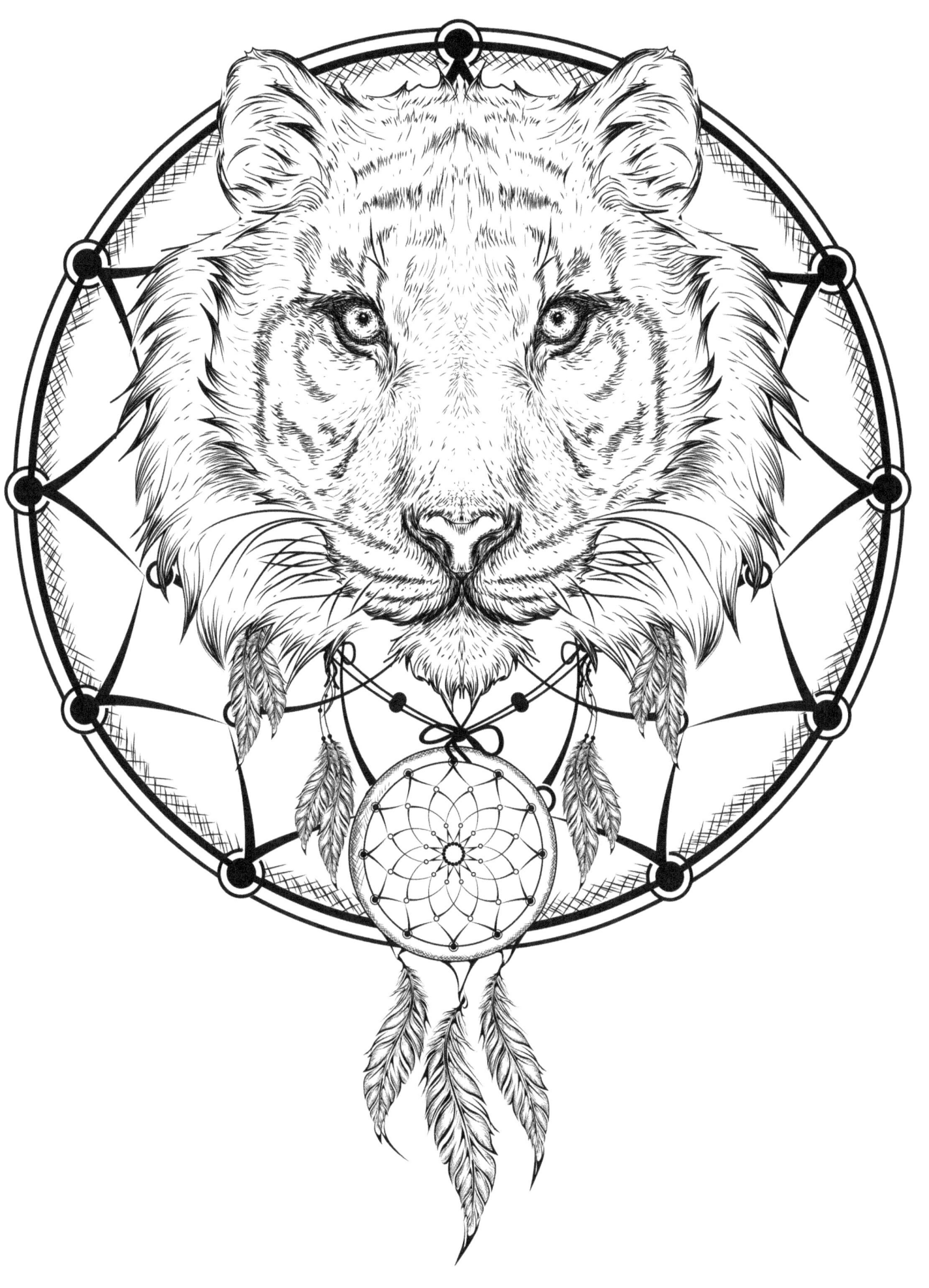

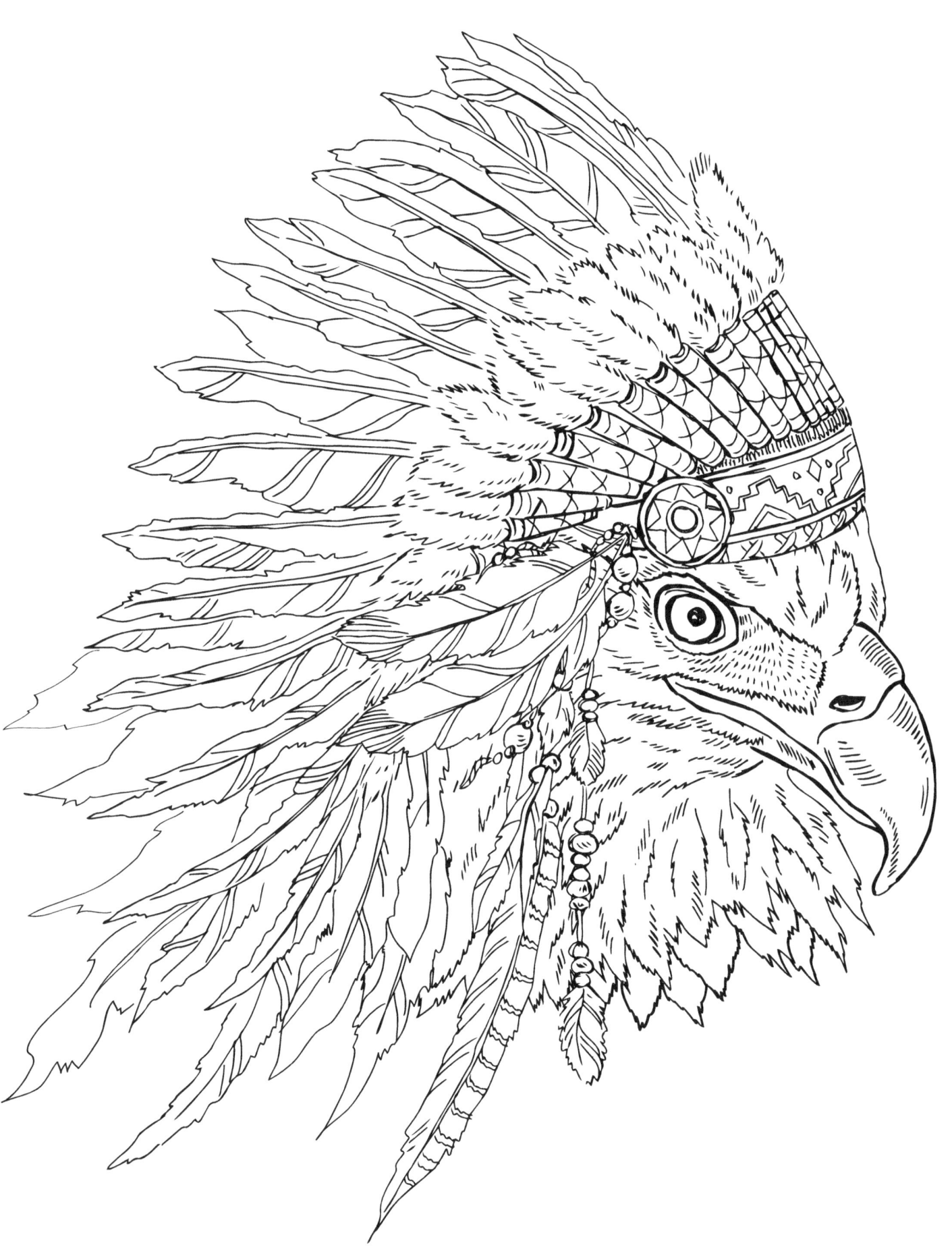

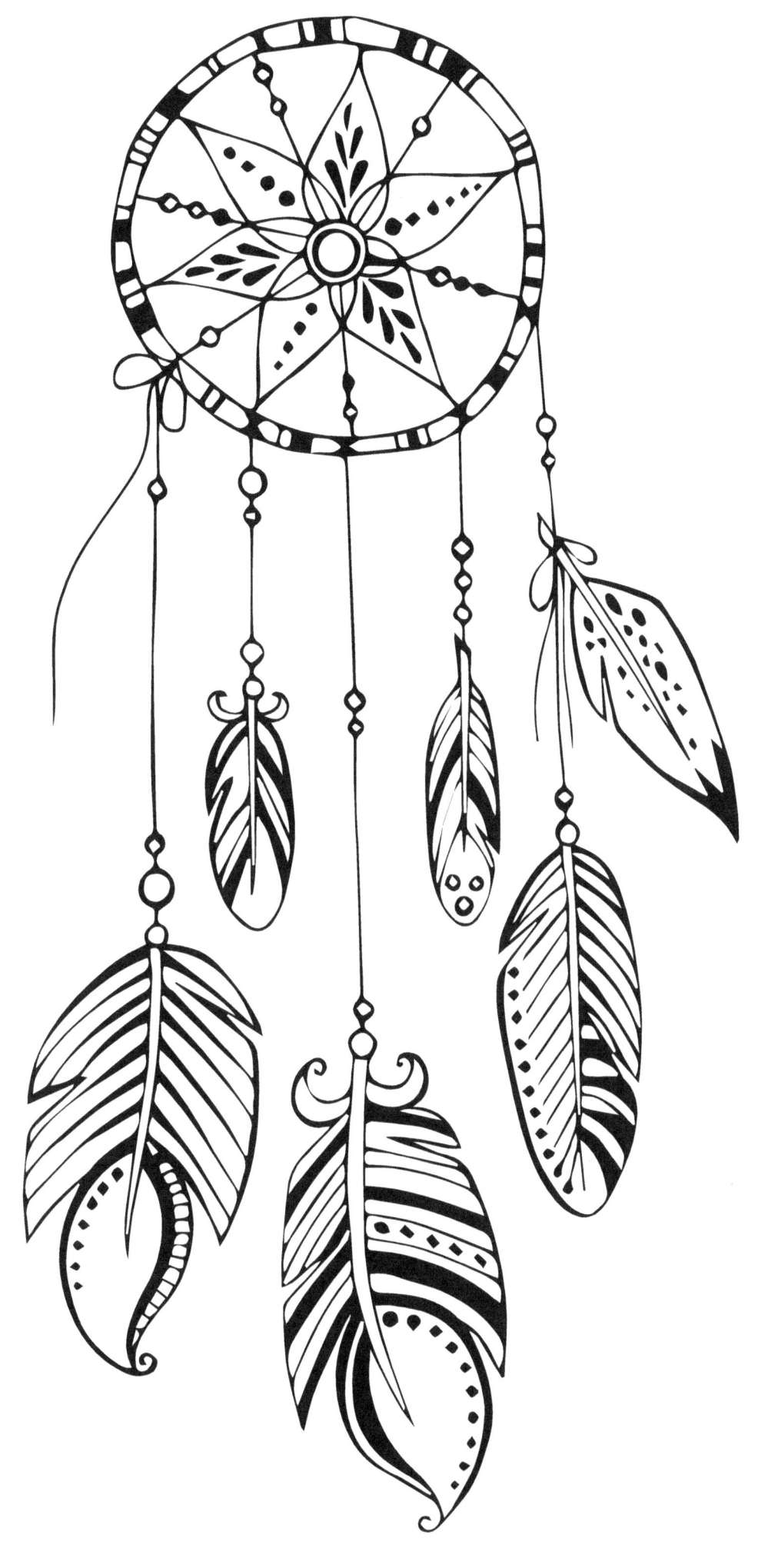

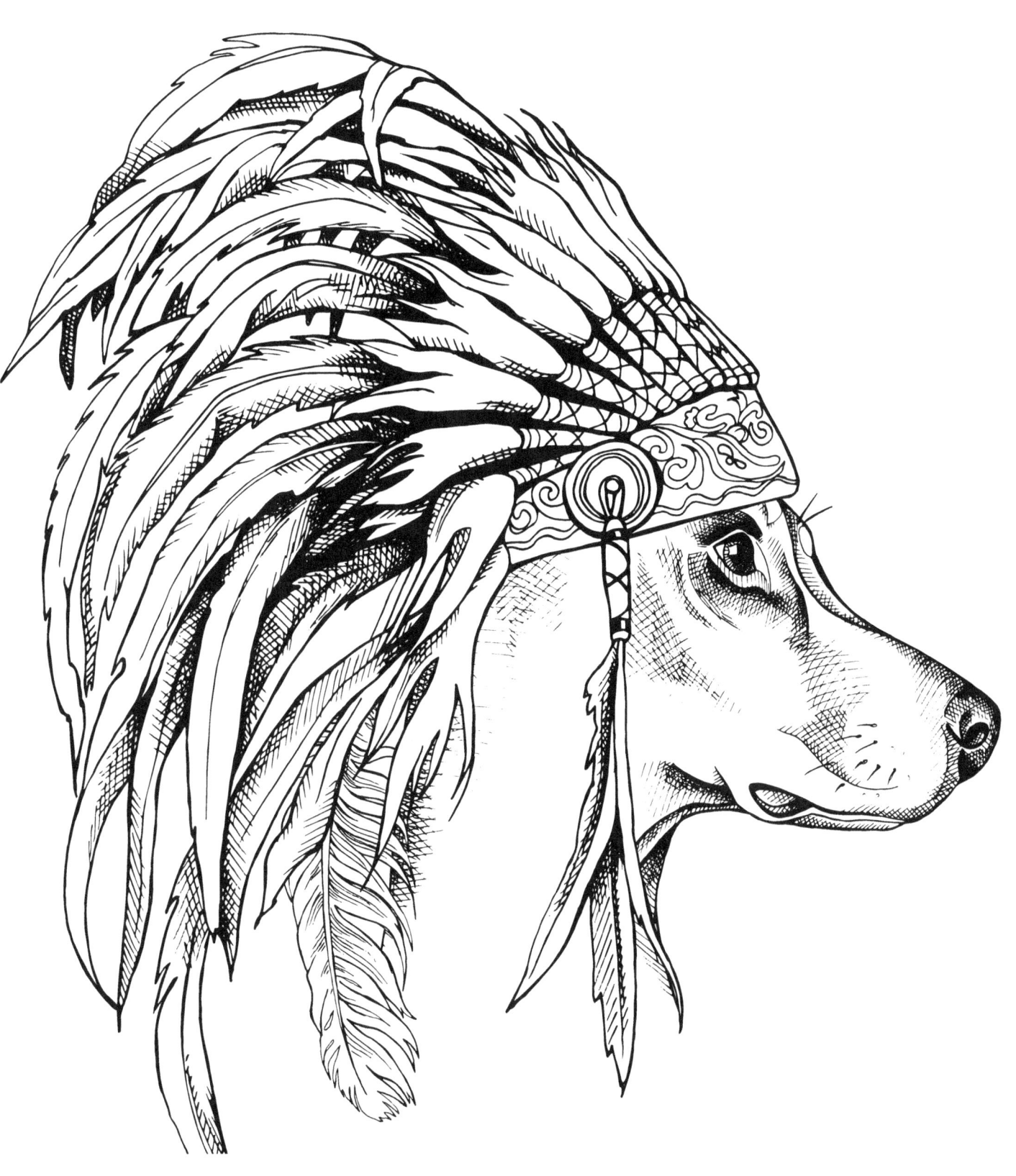

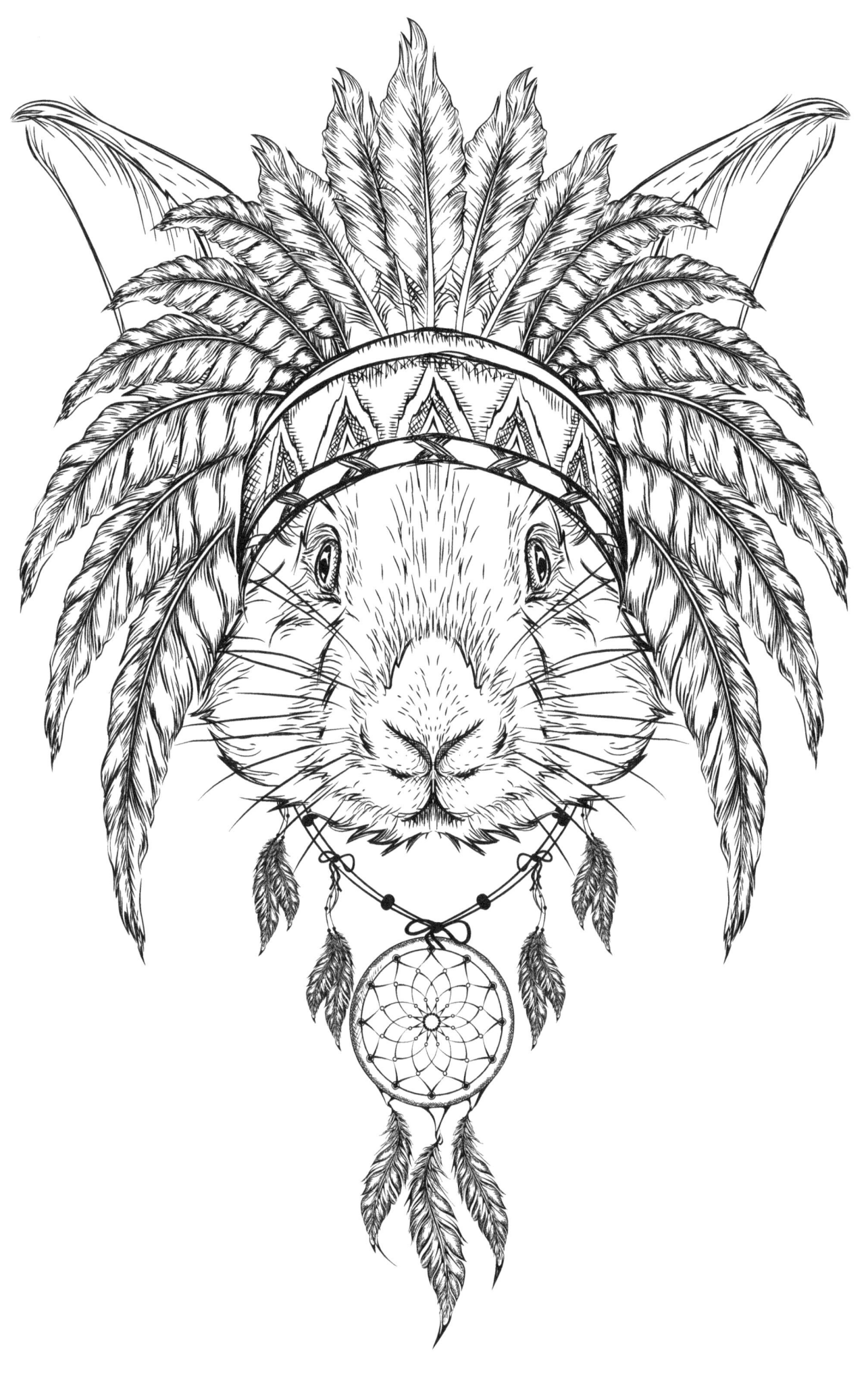

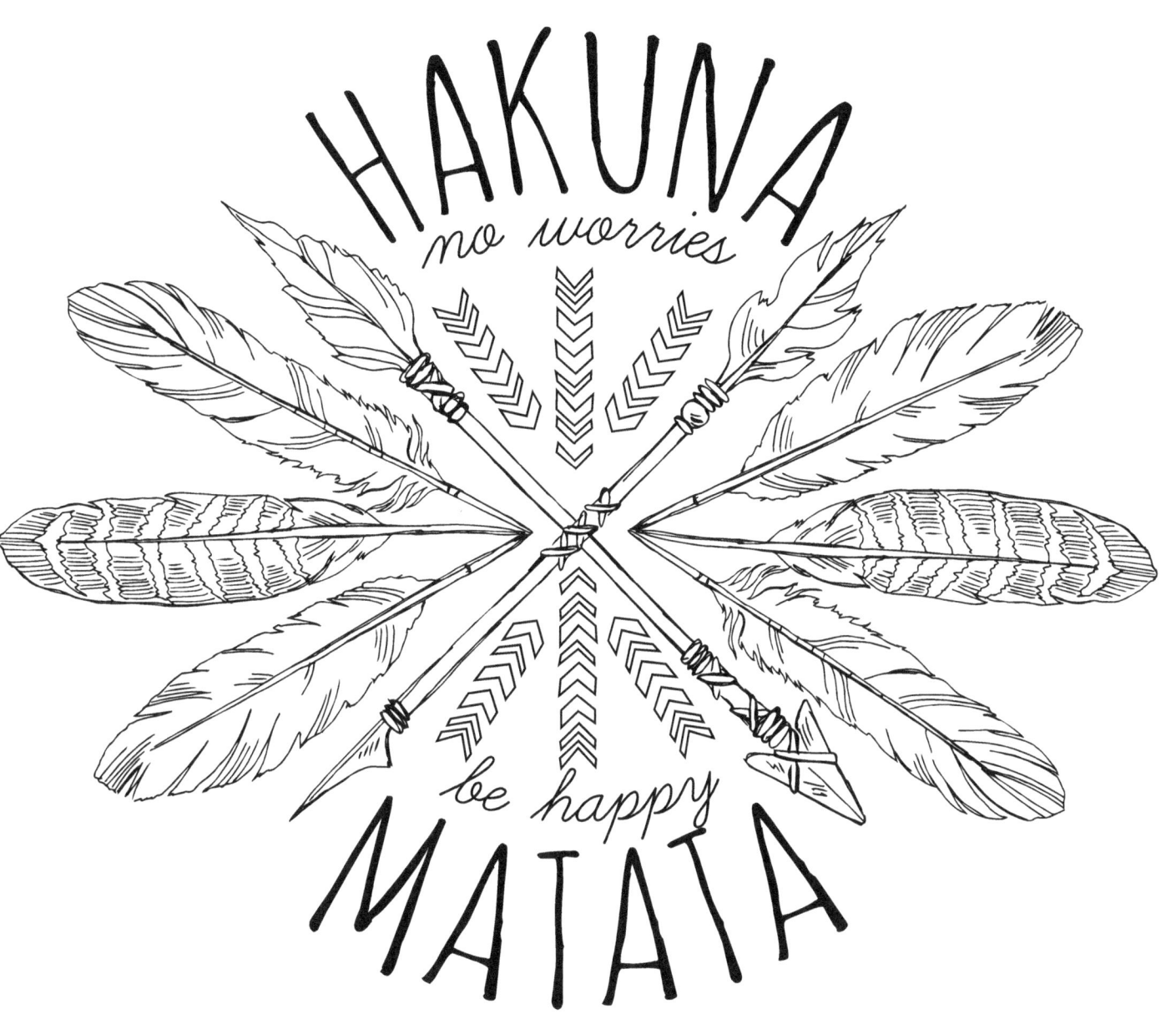

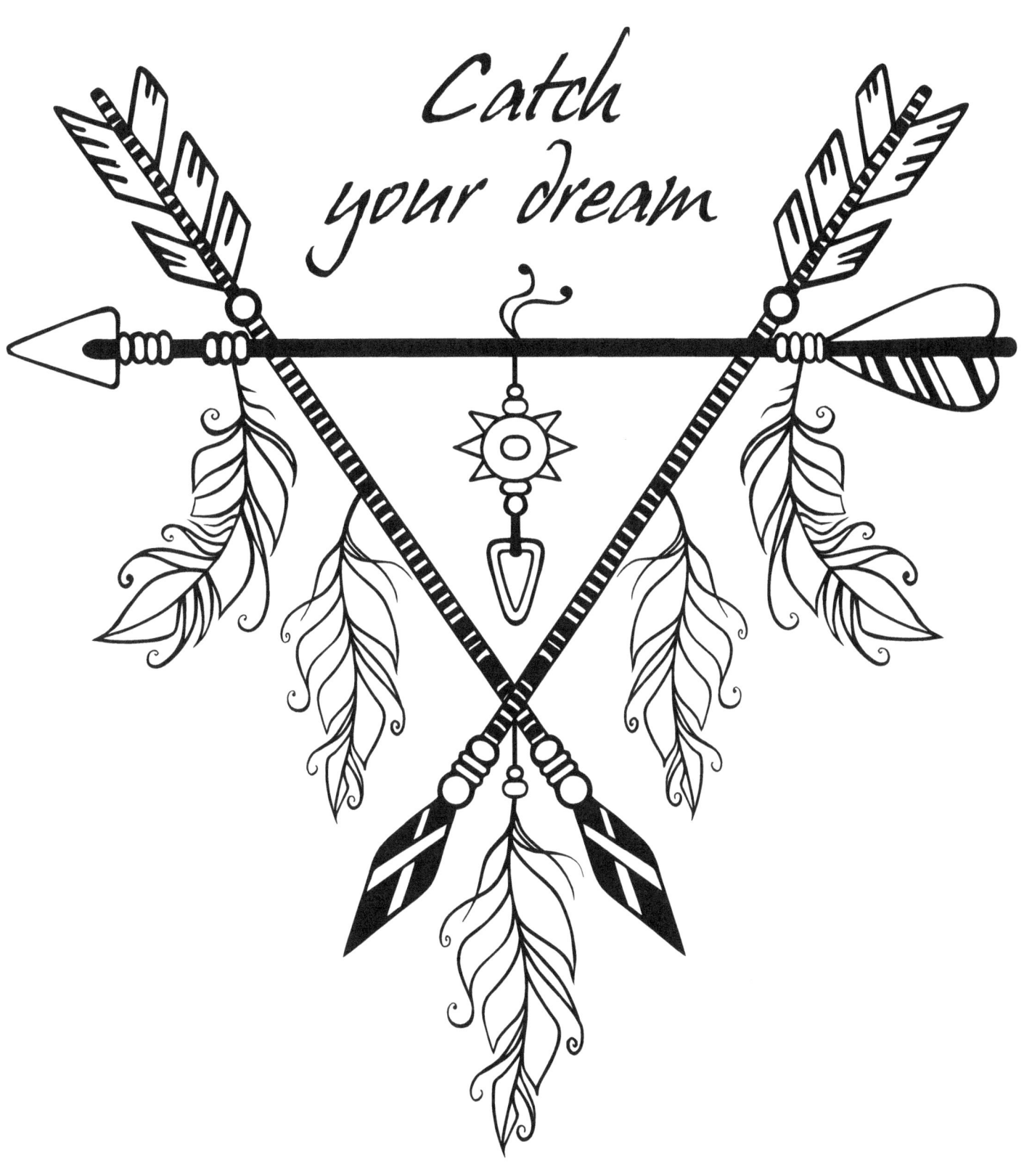

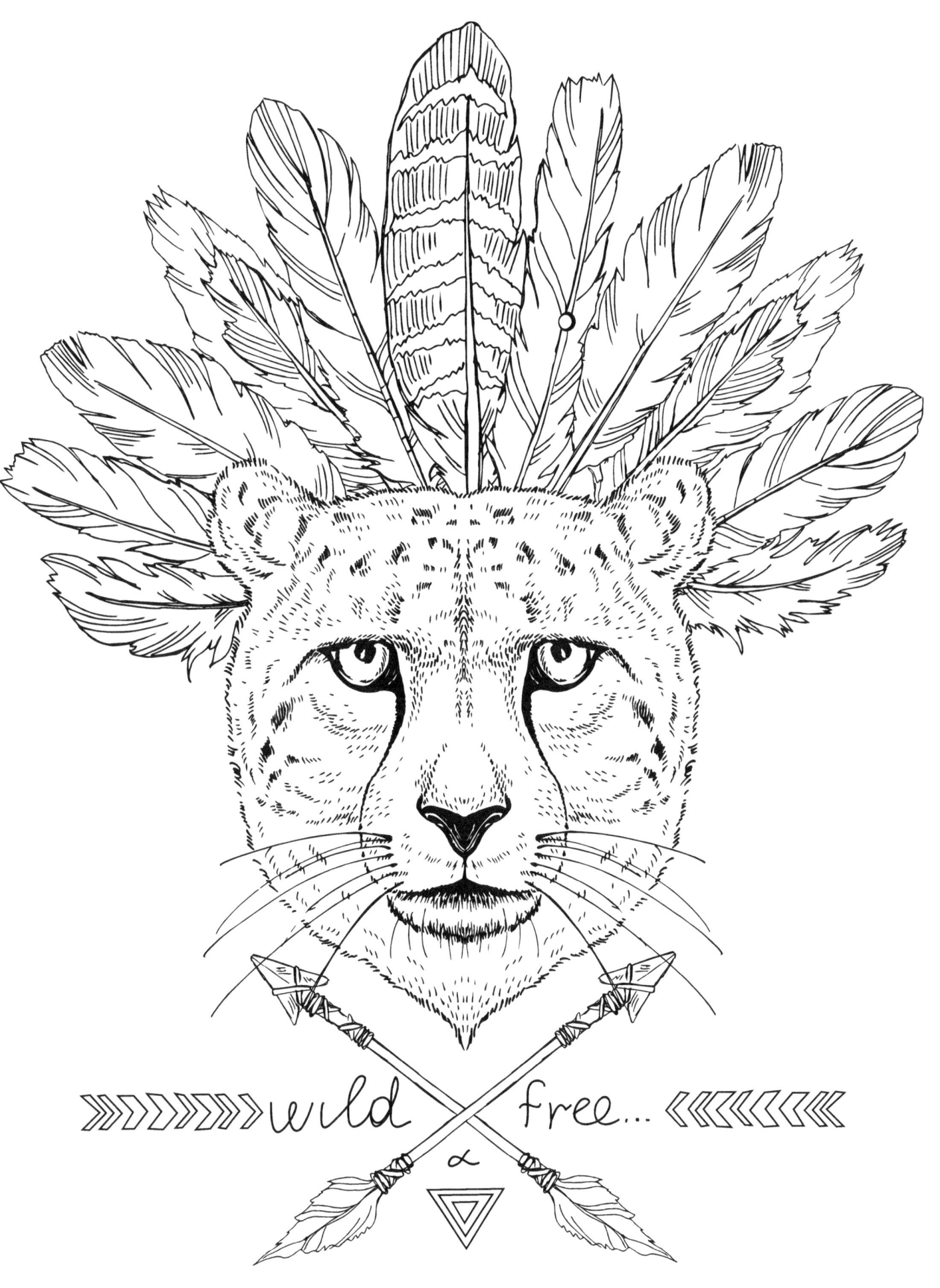

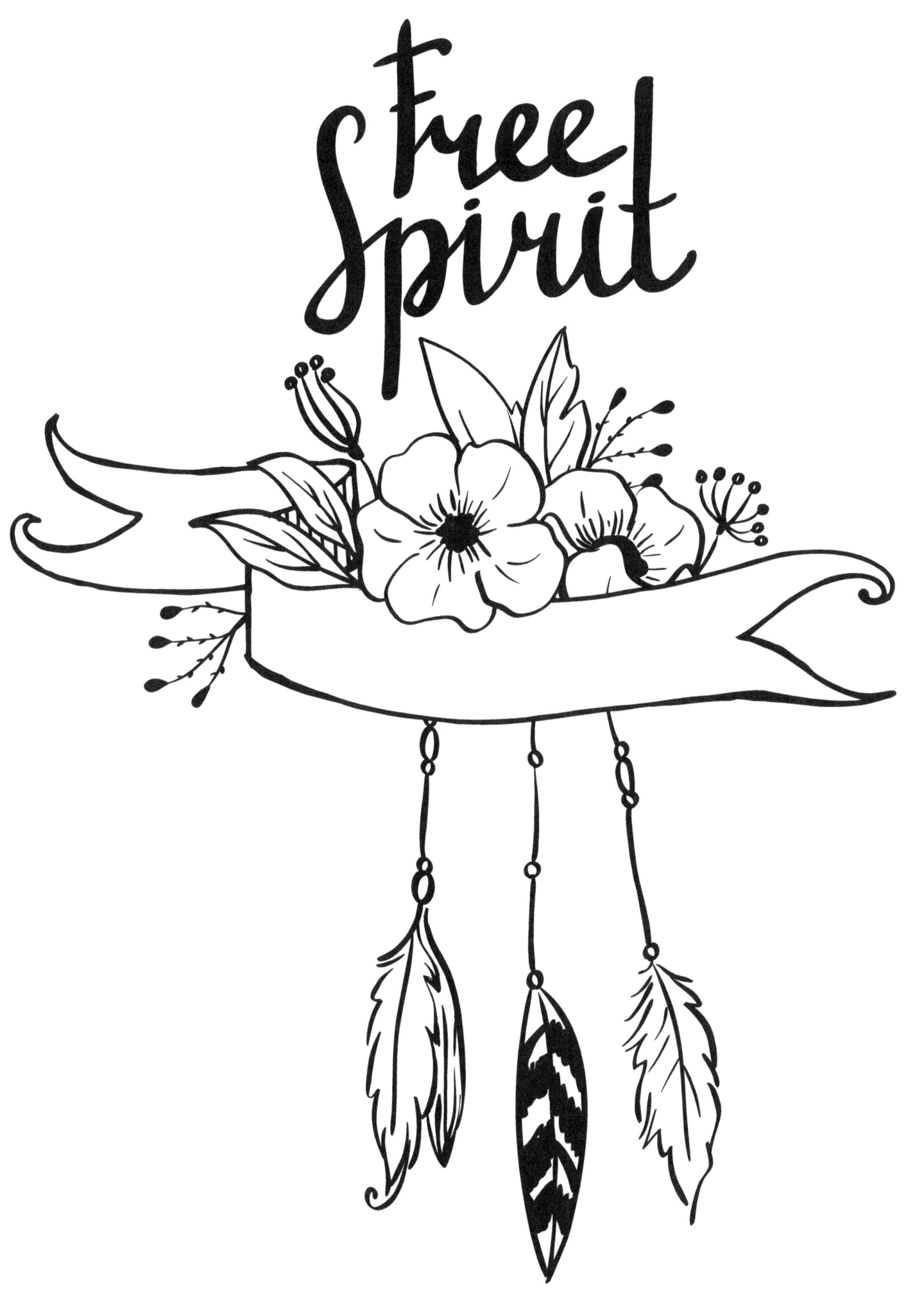

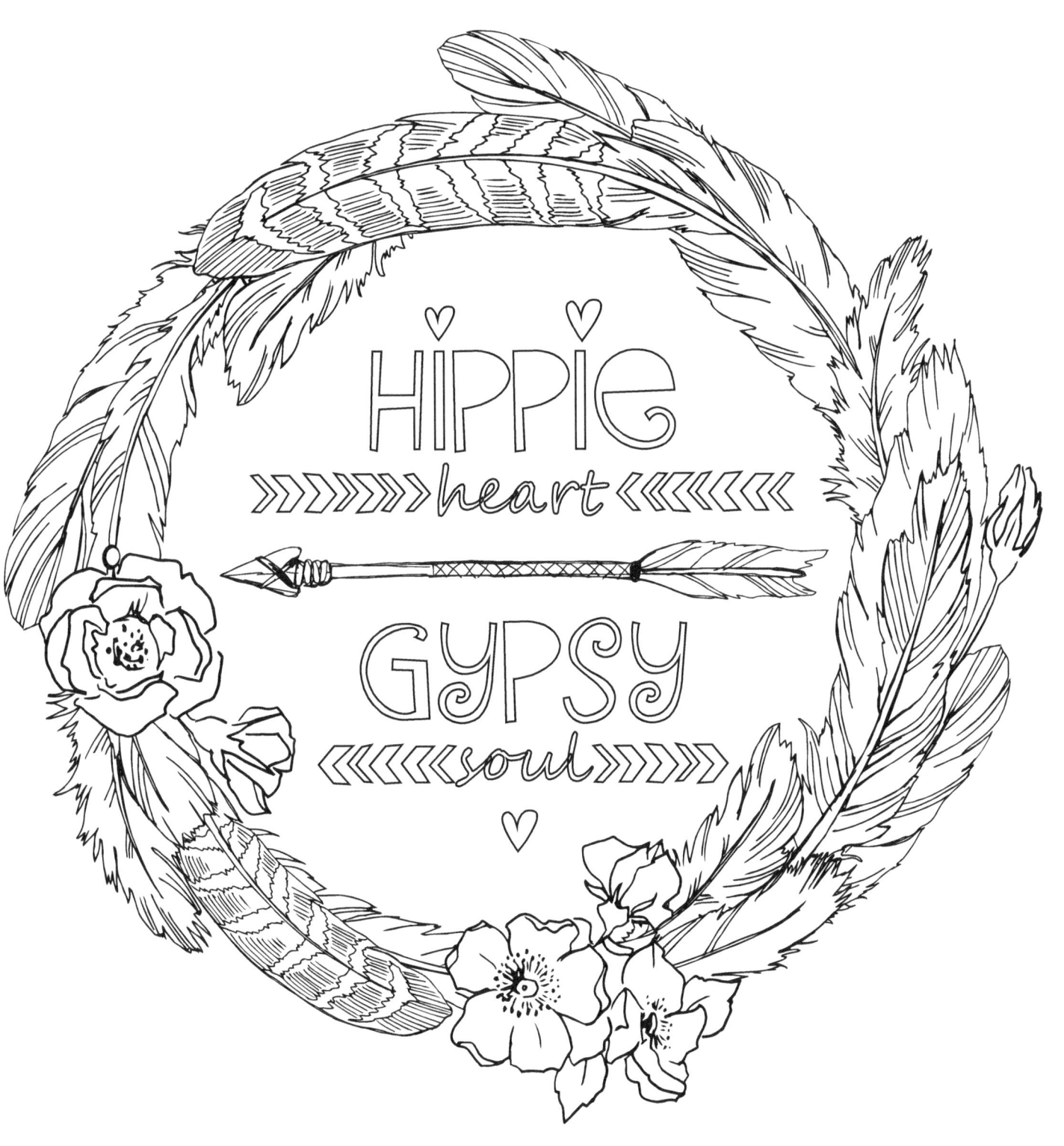

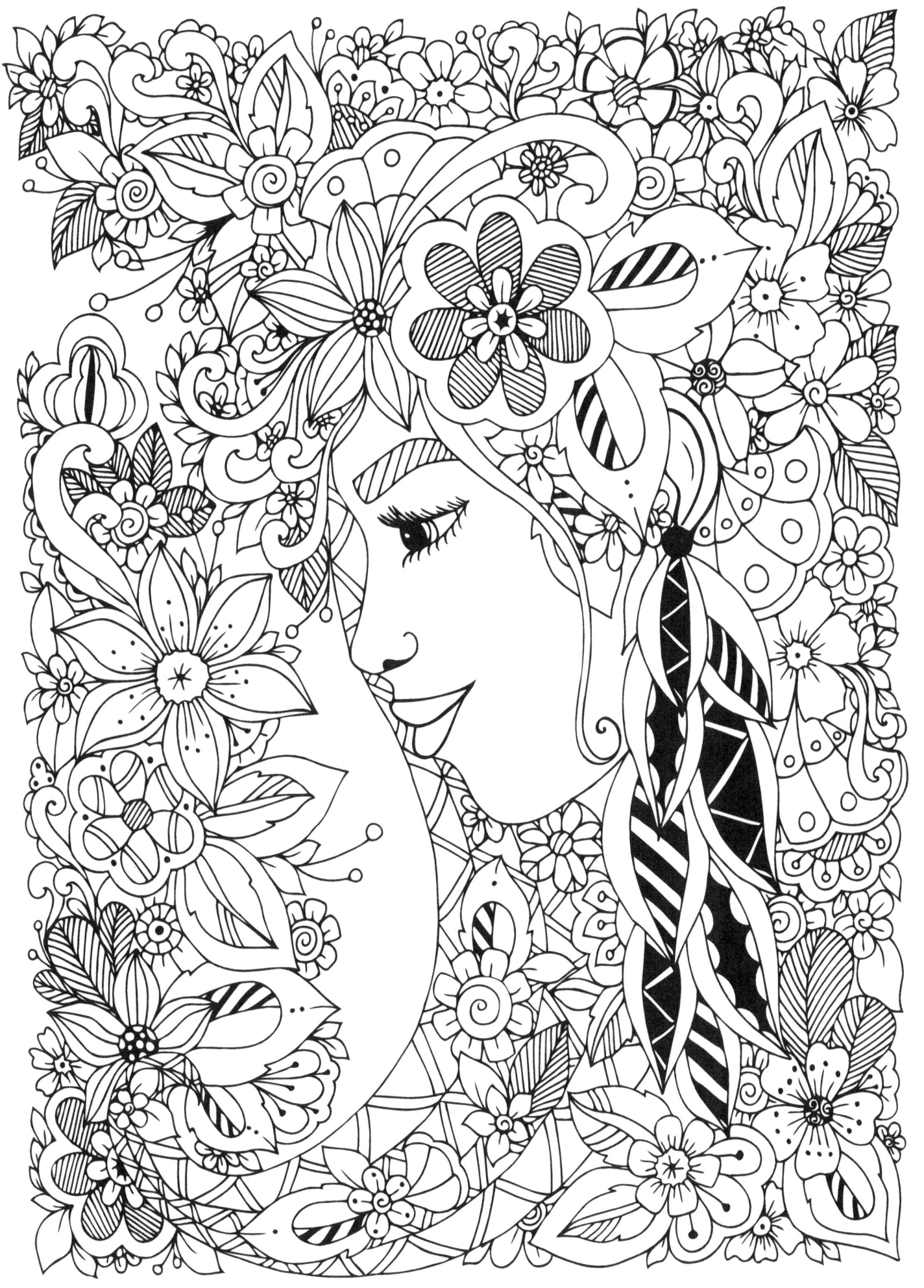

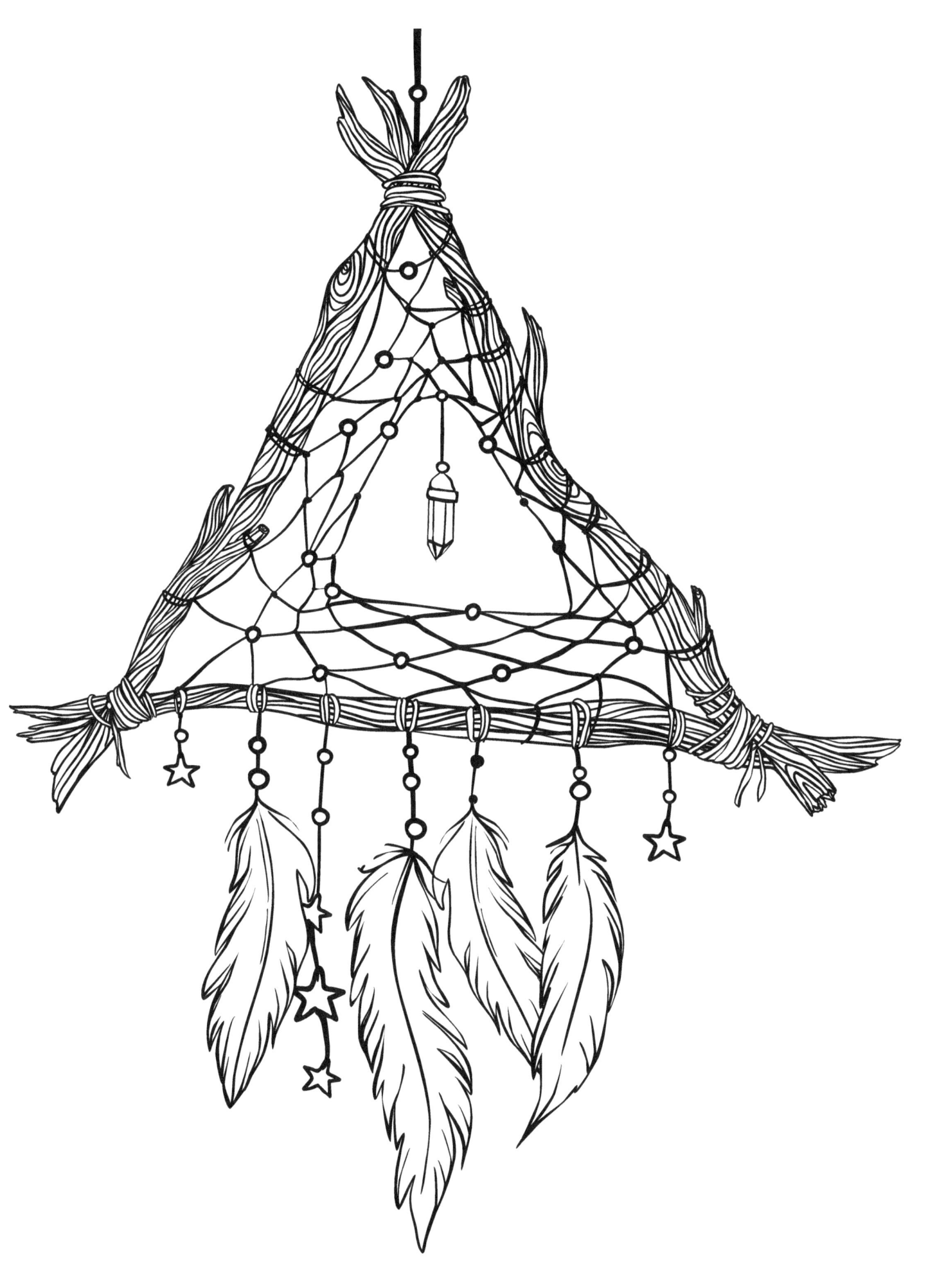

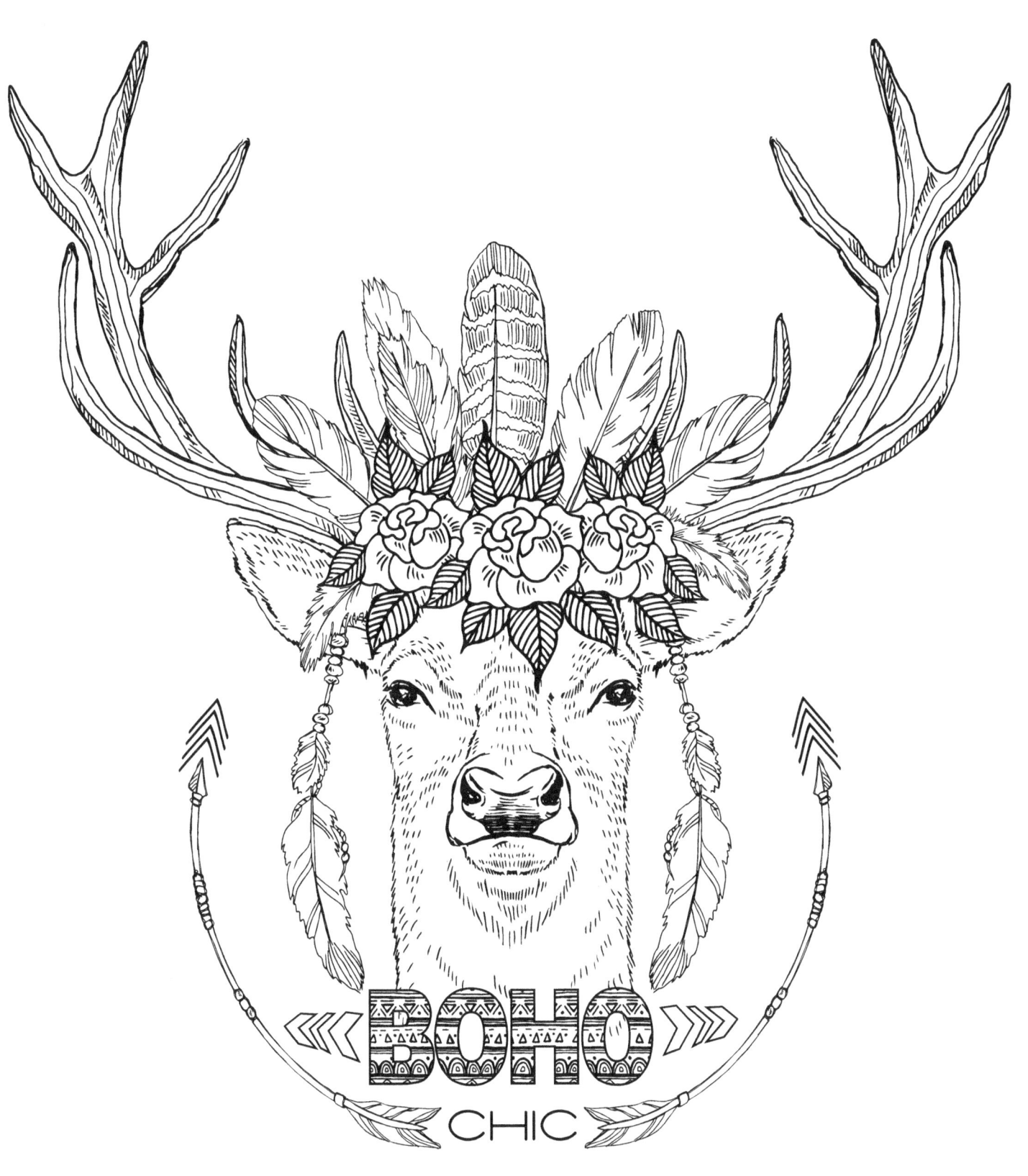

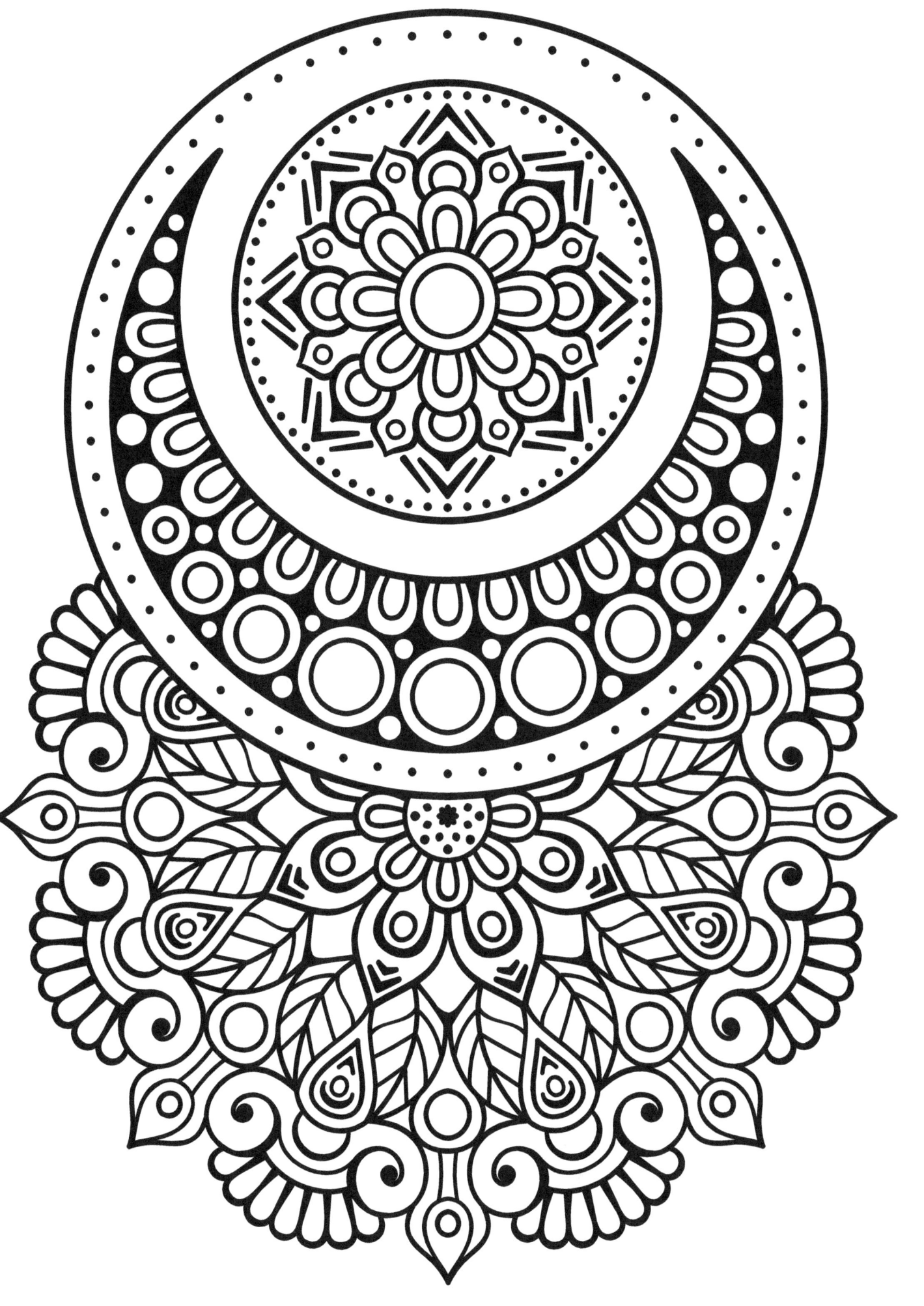

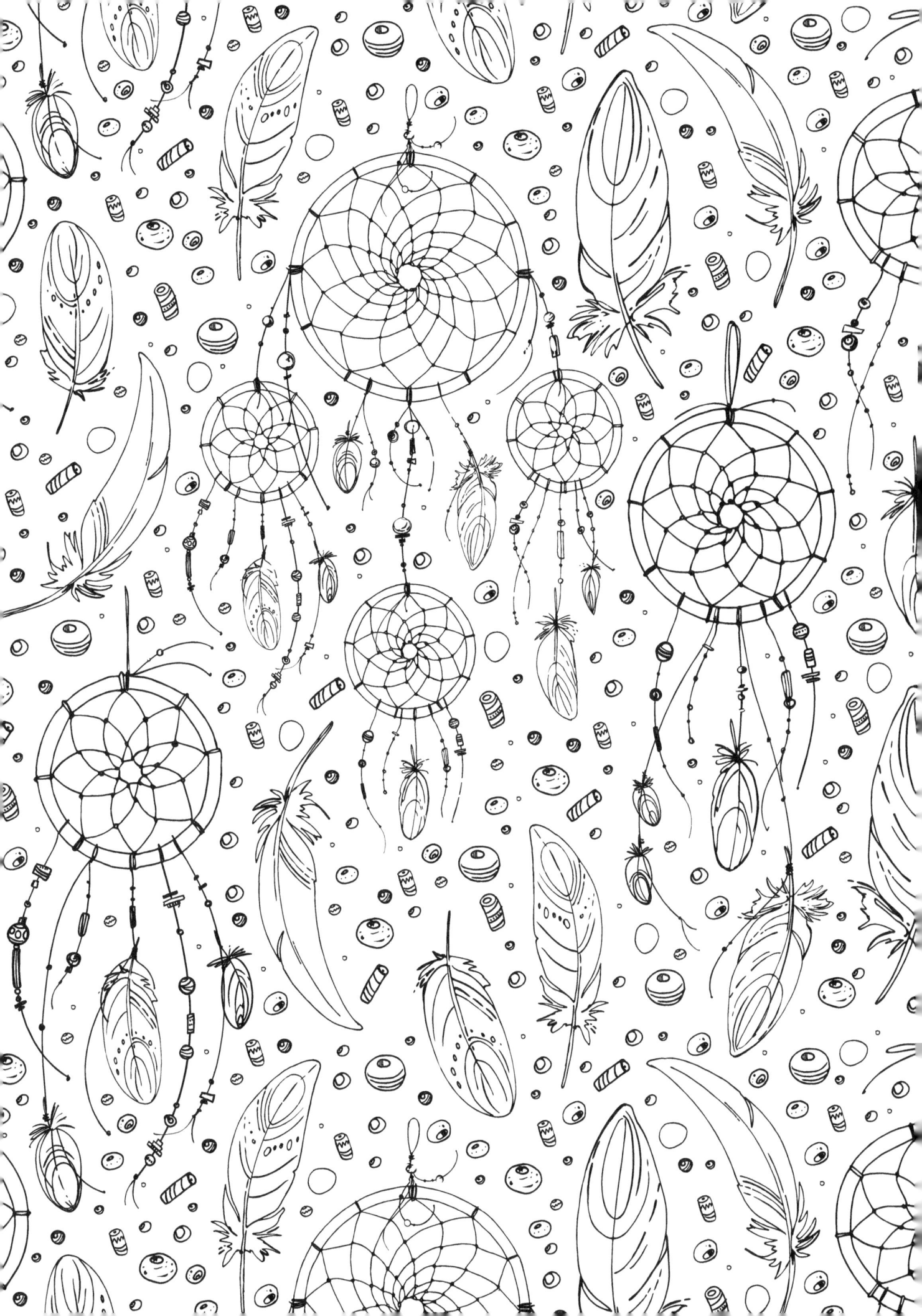

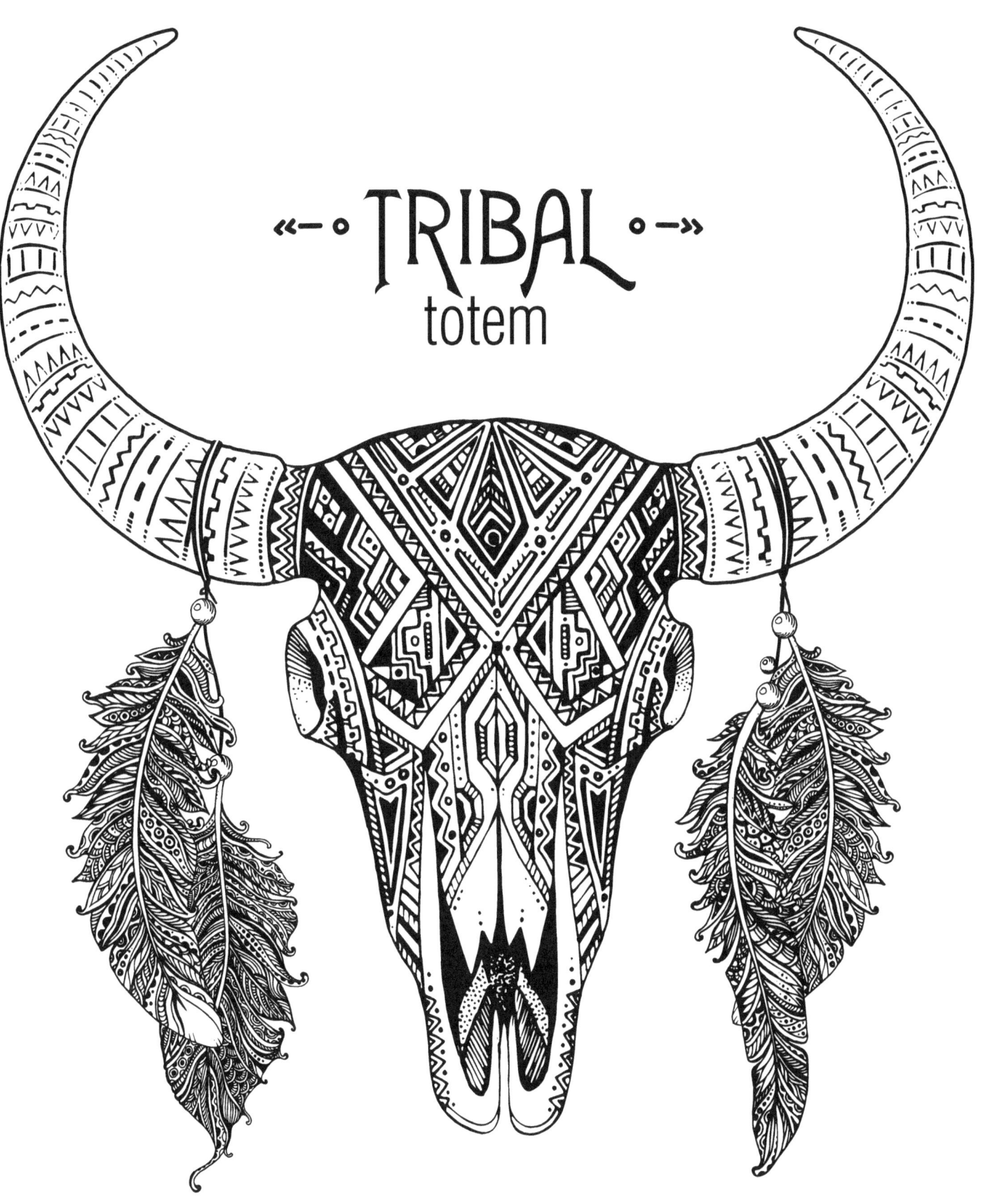

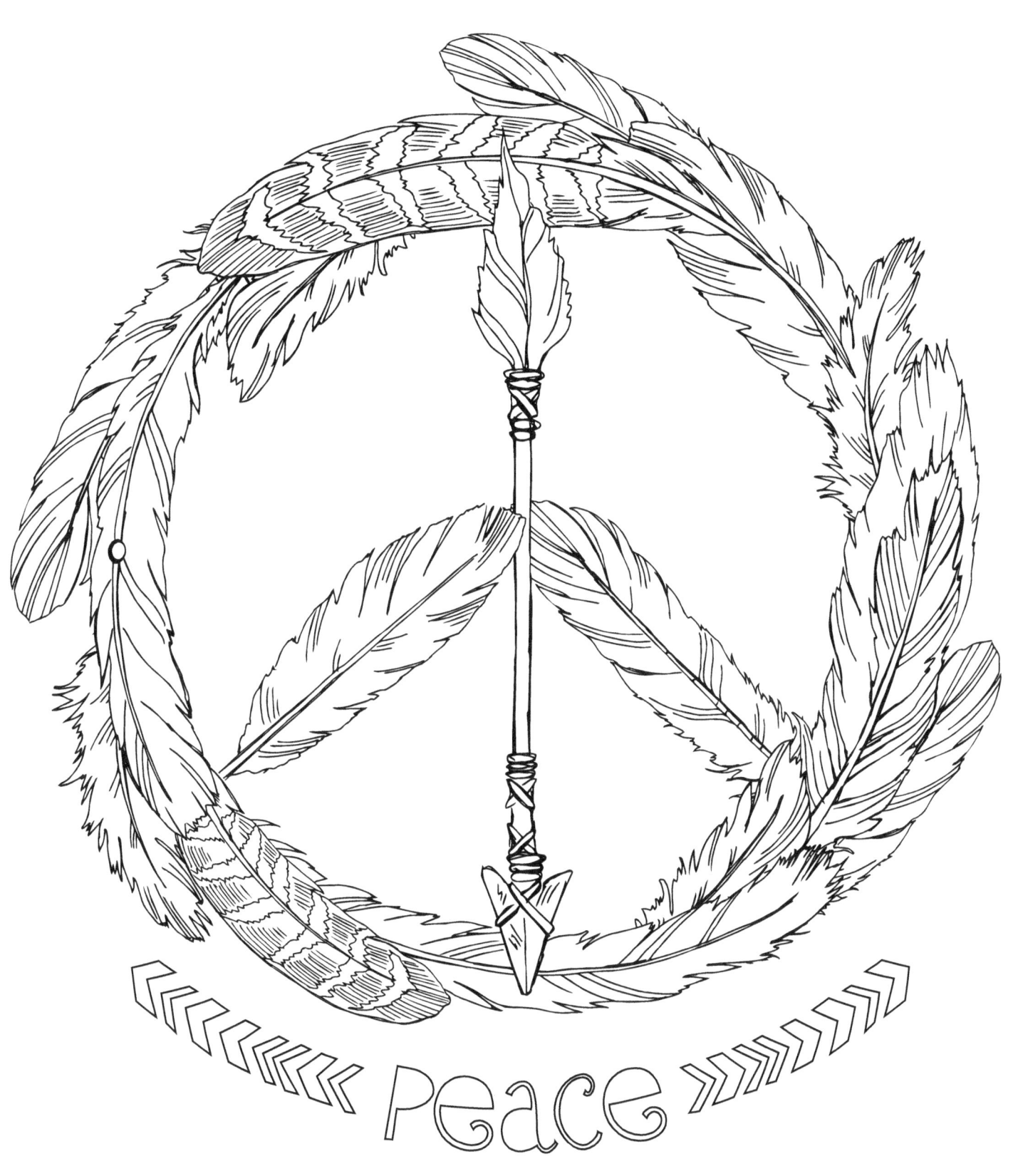

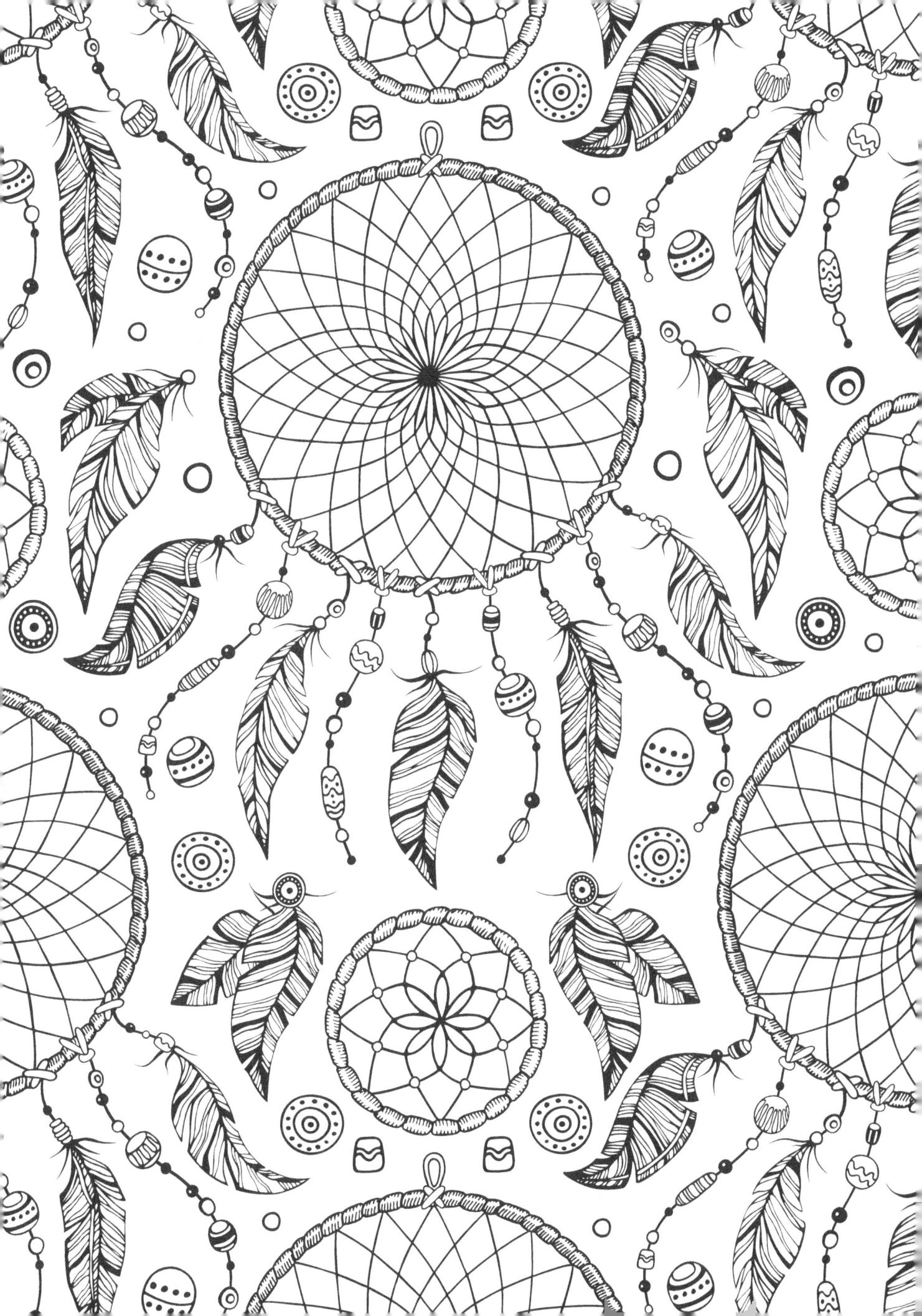

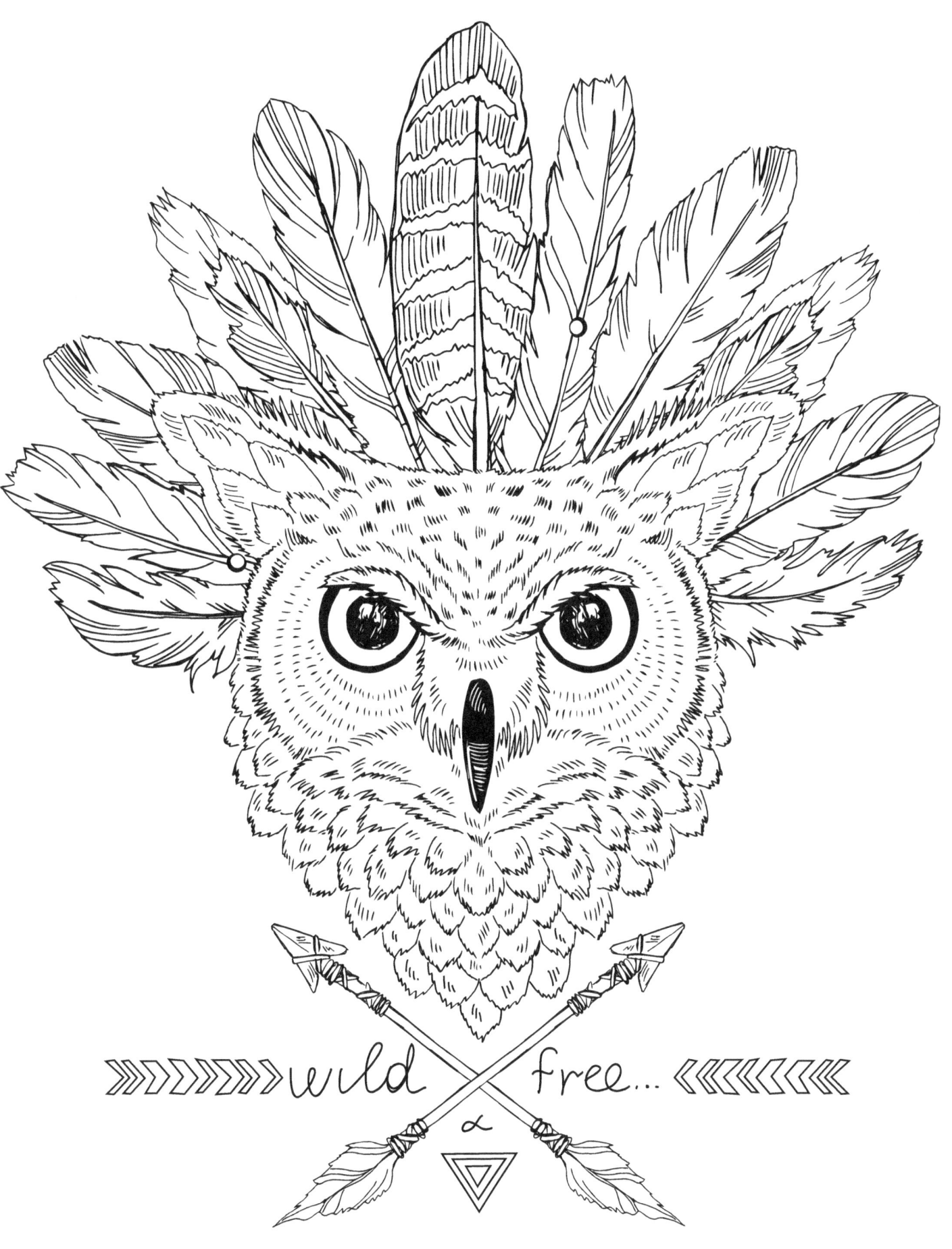

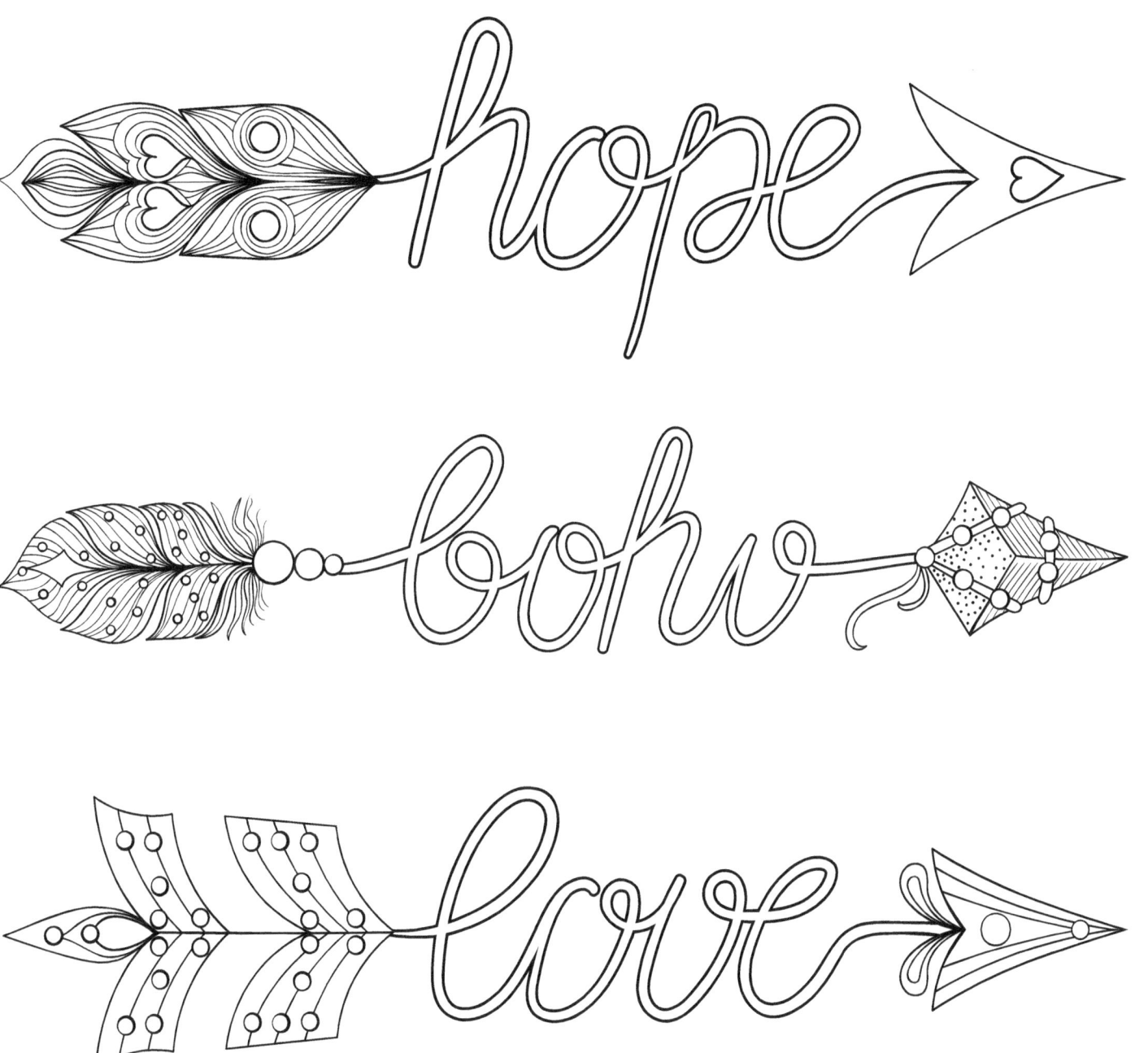

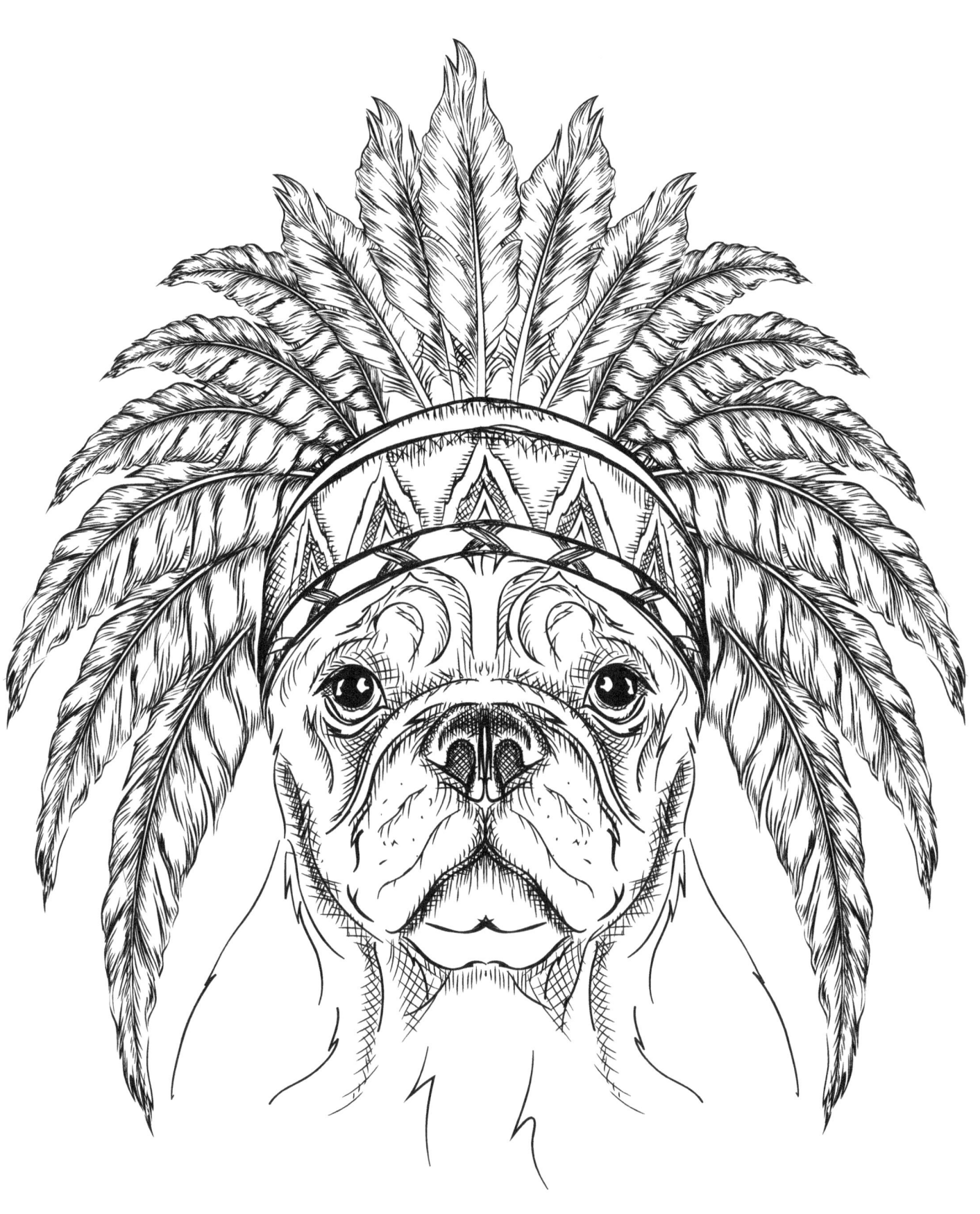

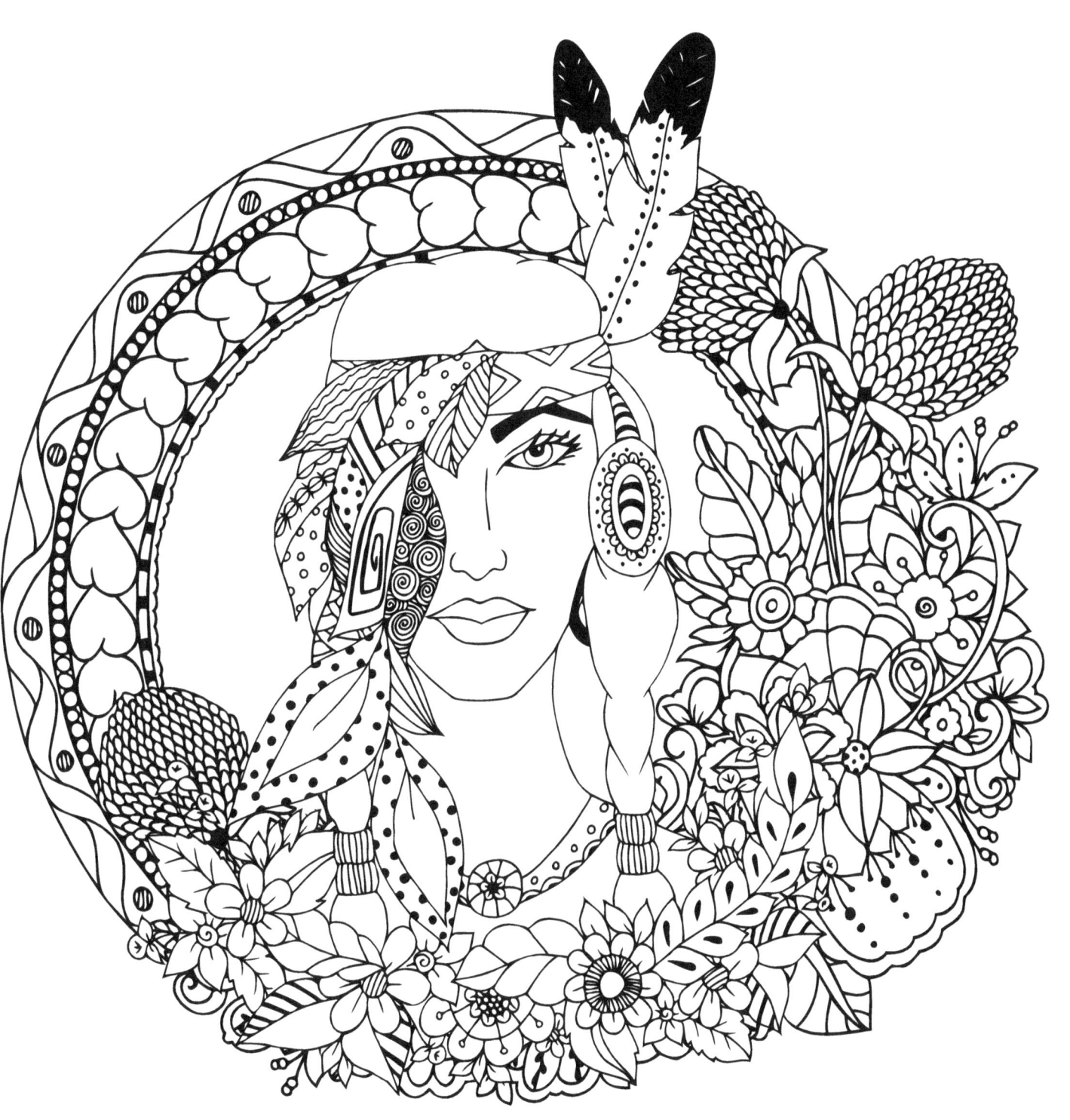

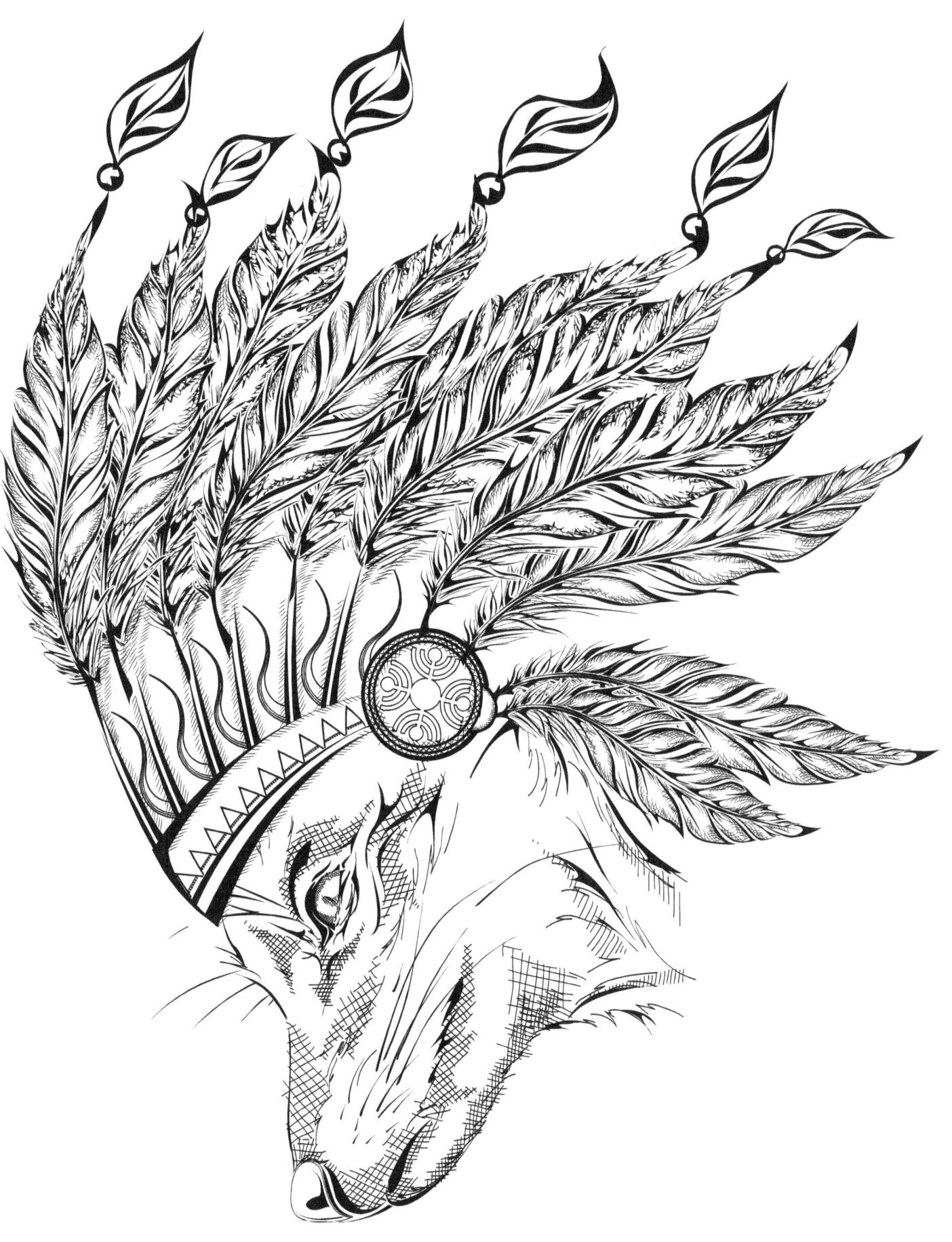

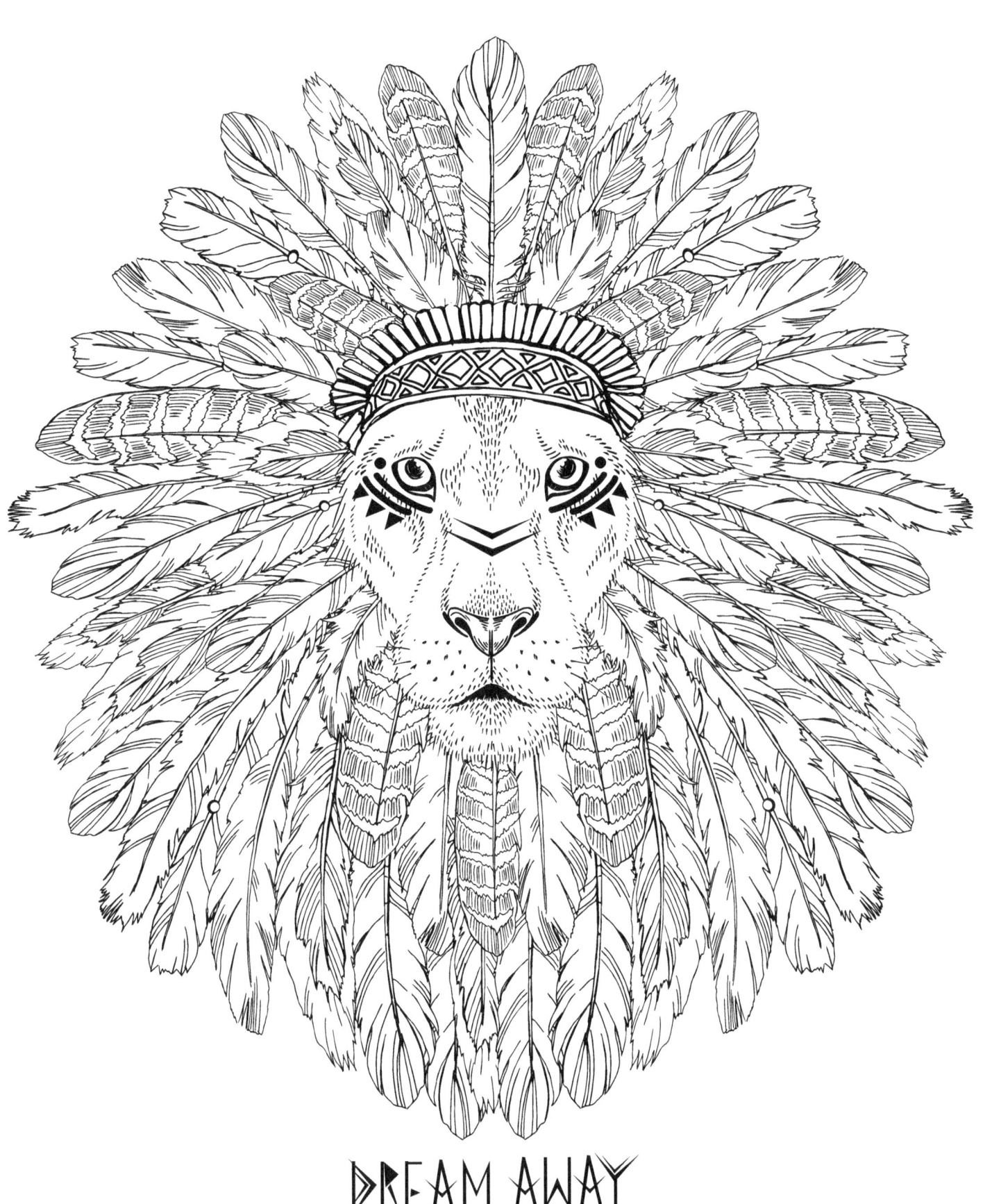

DREAM AWAY

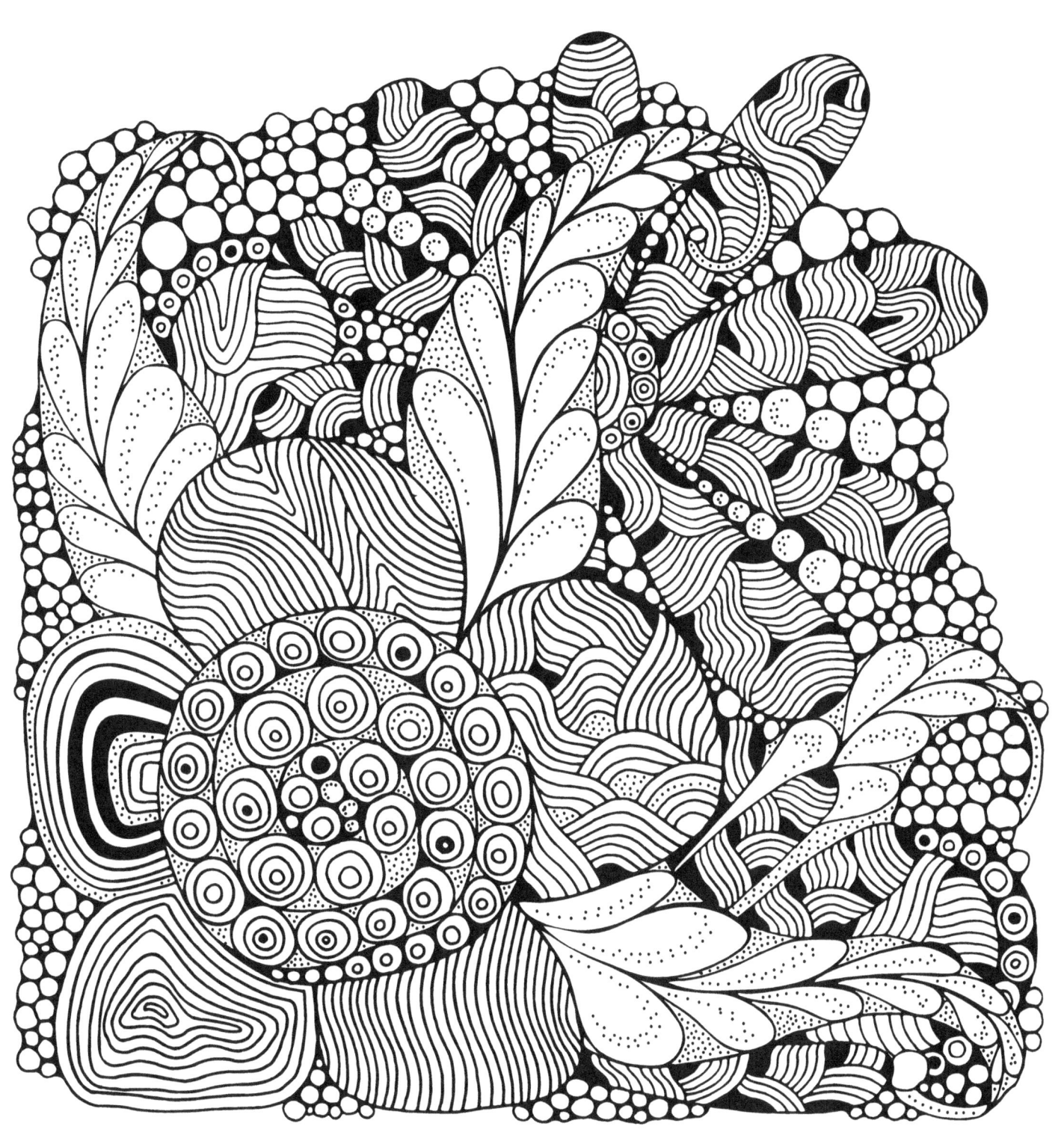

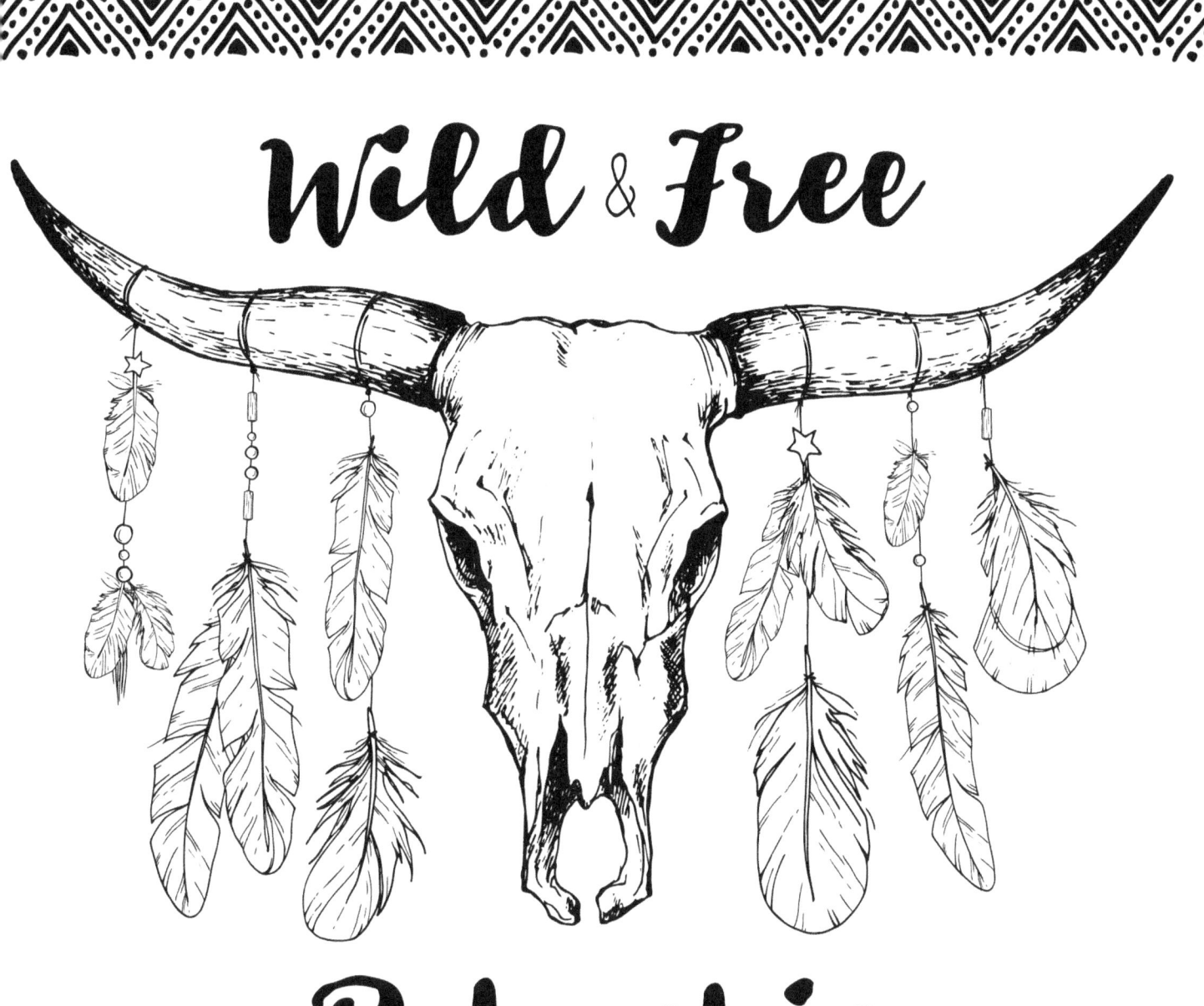

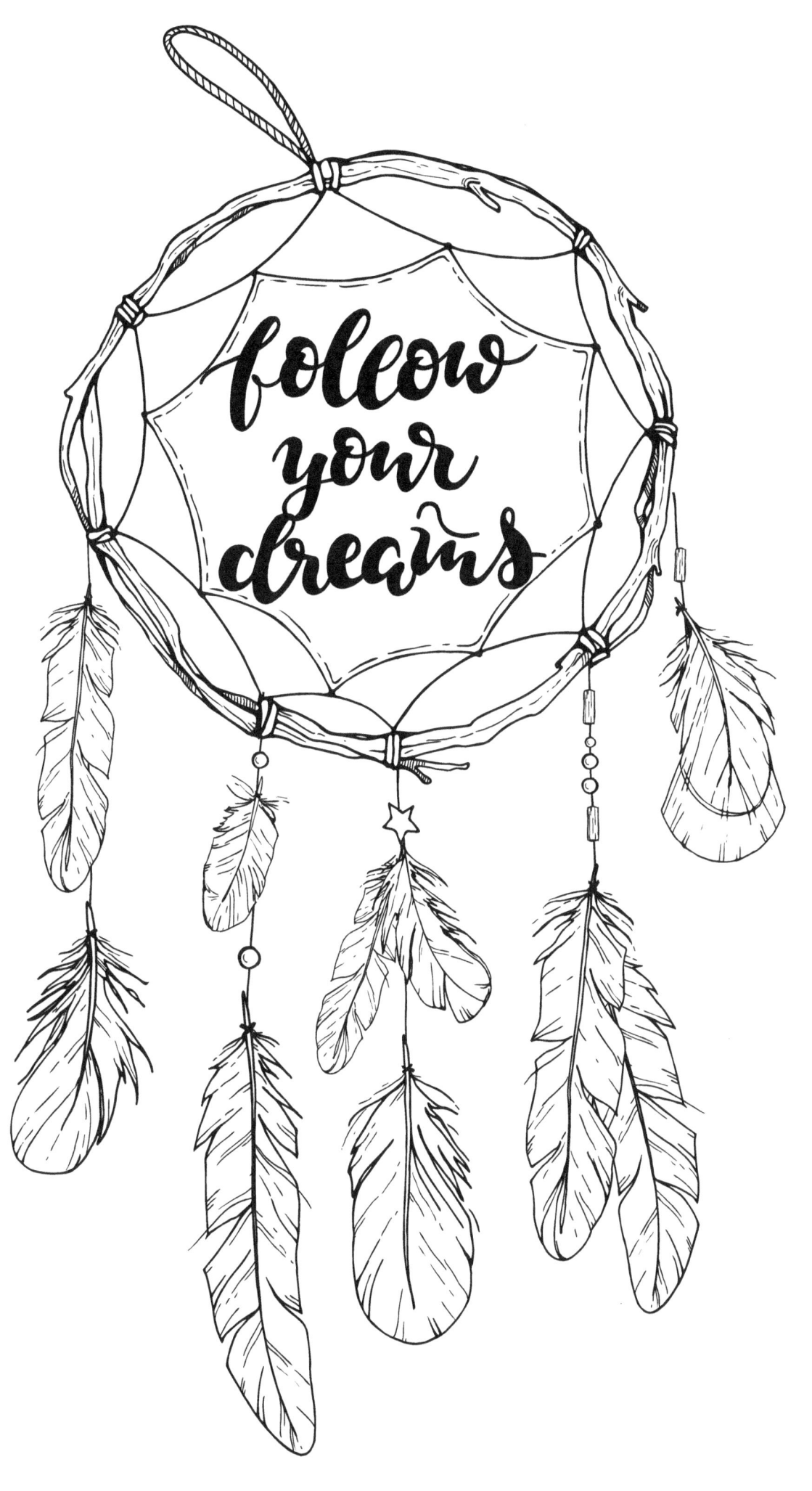

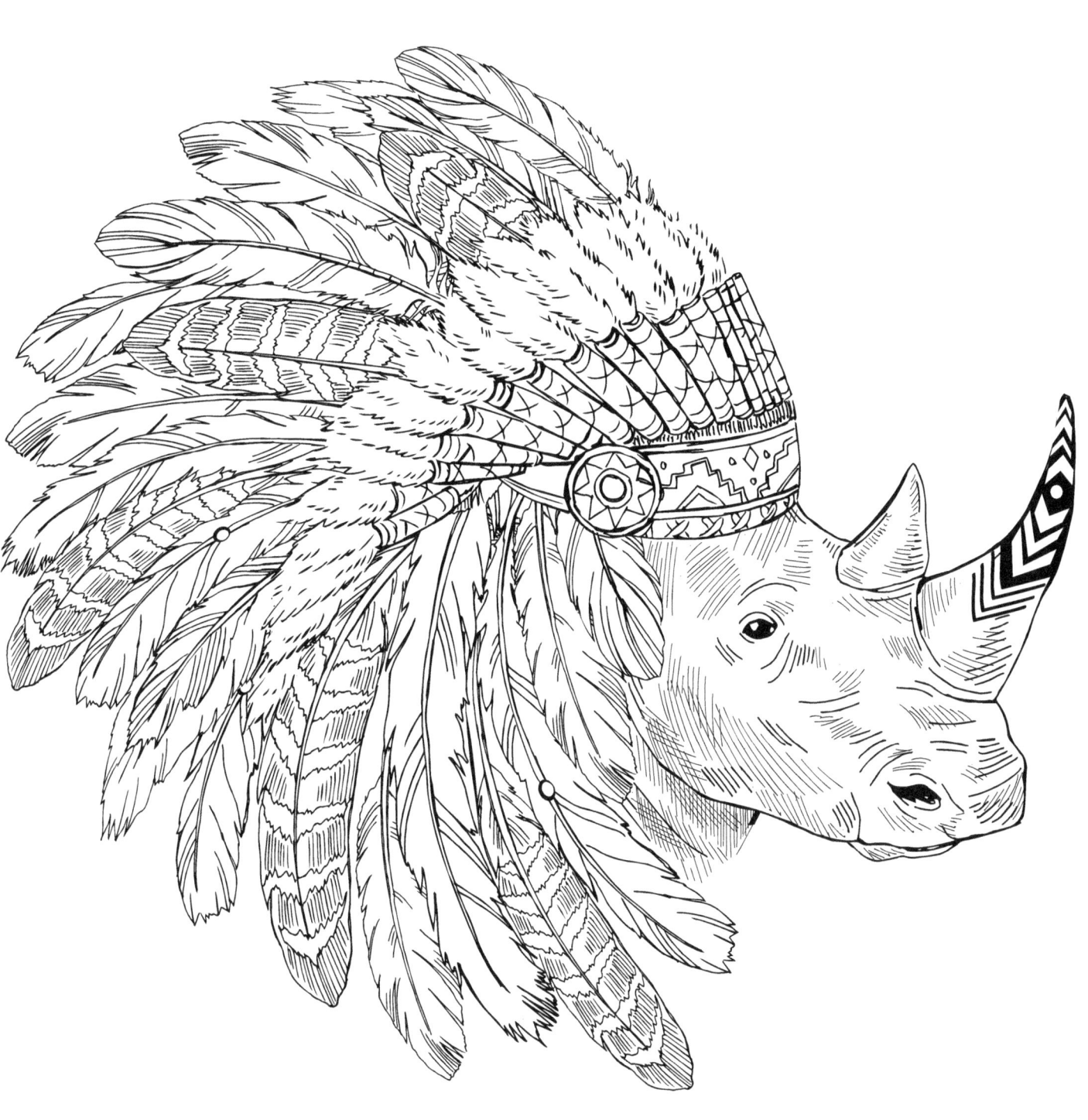

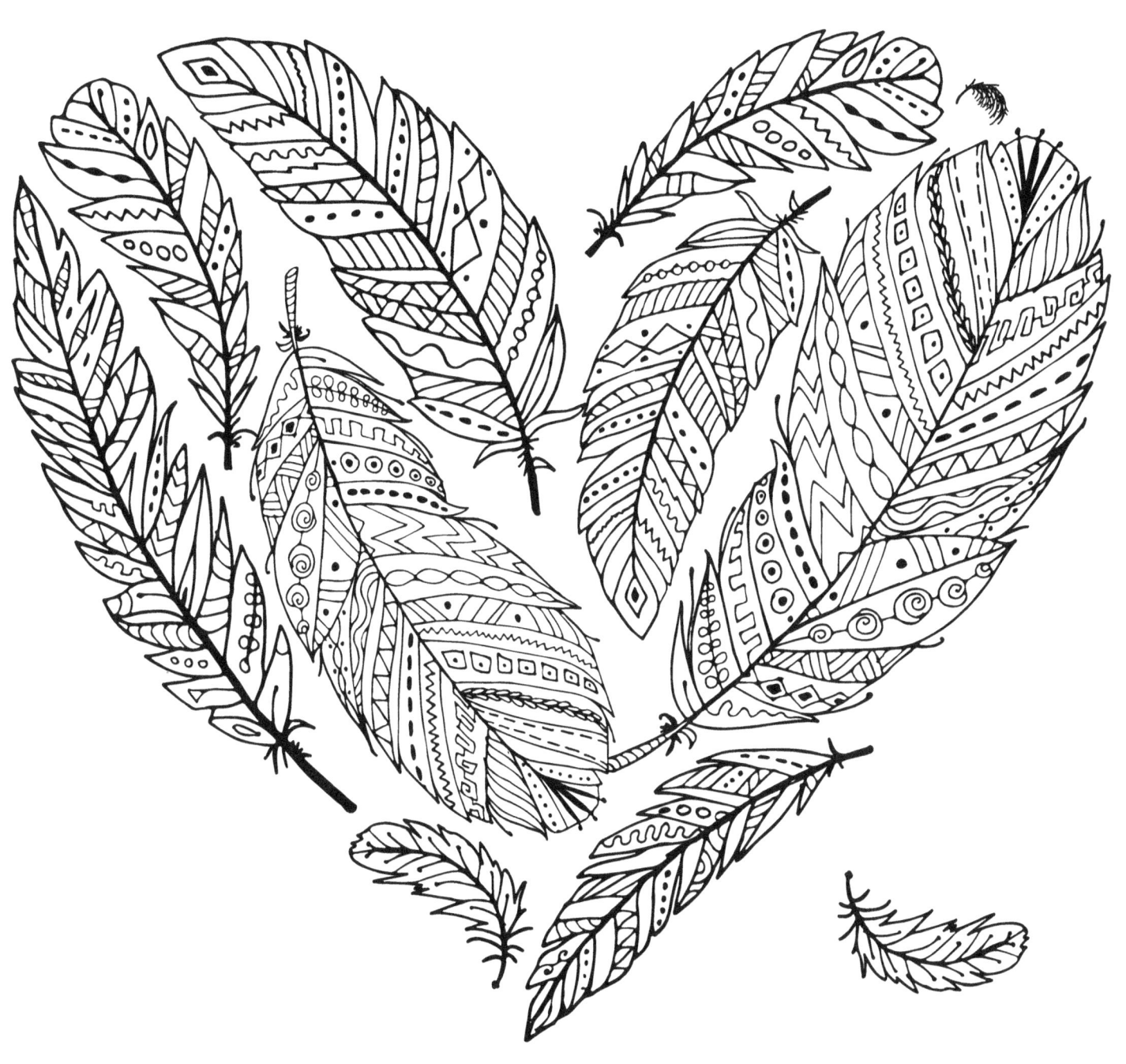

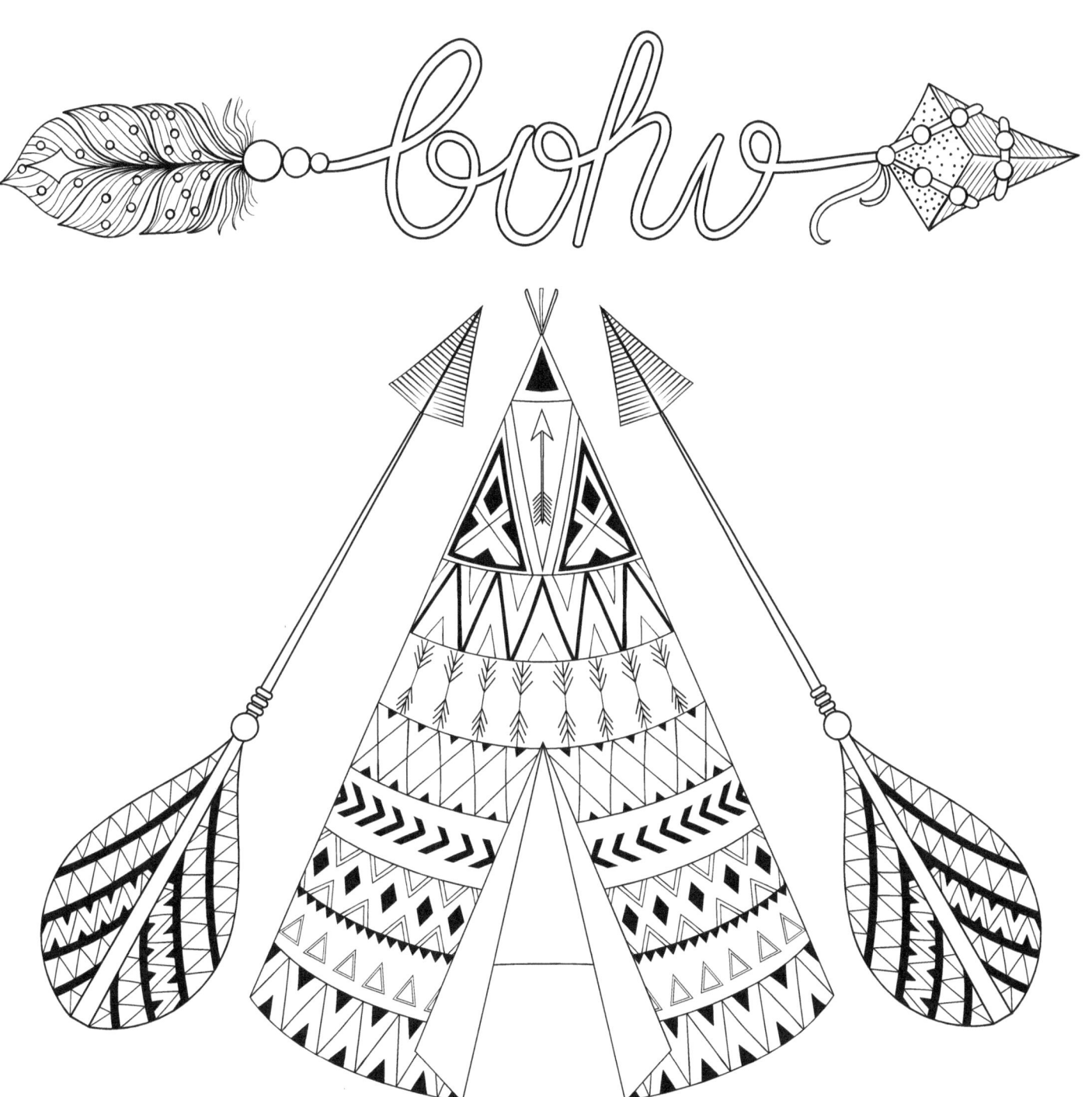

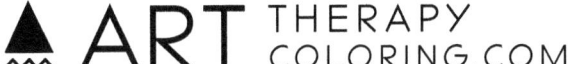

Drawings

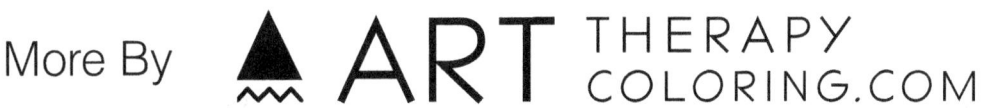
Best Selling Art Therapy Coloring Books

Coloring Books For Adults:

- Zombie Coloring Book: Black Background
- Butterfly Coloring Book For Adults: Black Background
- Tattoo Coloring Book: Black Background
- Coloring Books for Adults Relaxation: Native American Inspired Designs
- Fishing Coloring Book for Adults: Black Background

Coloring Books For Men:

- Coloring Book for Men: Anti-Stress Designs Vol 1
- Coloring Book For Men: Fishing Designs
- Coloring Book For Men: Tattoo Designs
- Coloring Books for Men: Hunting
- Coloring Book For Men: Biker Designs

Coloring Books For Seniors:

- Coloring Book For Seniors: Nature Designs Vol 1
- Coloring Book For Seniors: Anti-Stress Designs Vol 1
- Coloring Books for Seniors: Relaxing Designs
- Coloring Book For Seniors: Floral Designs Vol 1
- Coloring Book For Seniors: Ocean Designs Vol 1

Coloring Books For Teens and Tweens:

- Coloring Books For Teens: Ocean Designs
- Coloring Books for Teen Girls Vol 1
- Teen Inspirational Coloring Books
- Coloring Book for Teens: Anti-Stress Designs Vol 1
- Tween Coloring Books For Girls: Cute Animals

Coloring Books For Kids:

- Horse Coloring Book For Girls
- Coloring Books For Boys: Sharks
- Coloring Books for Boys: Animal Designs
- Unicorn Coloring Book for Girls
- Detailed Coloring Books For Kids

Art Therapy Coloring Books

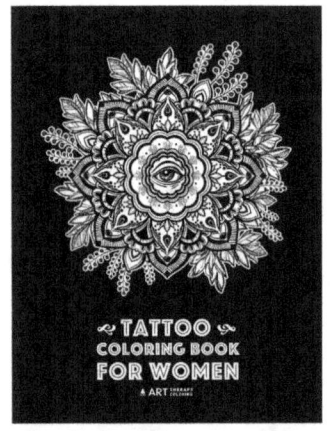

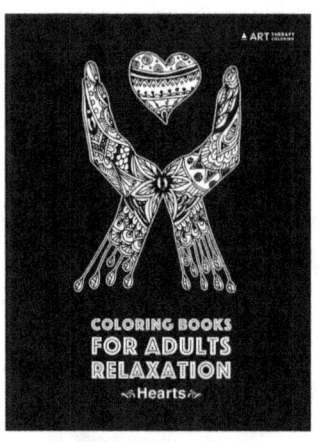

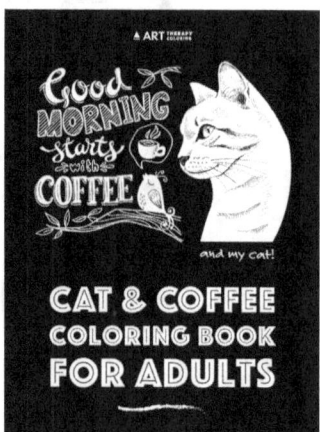

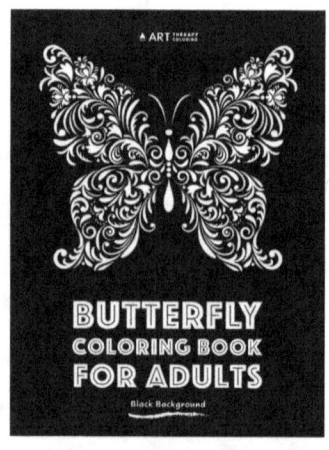

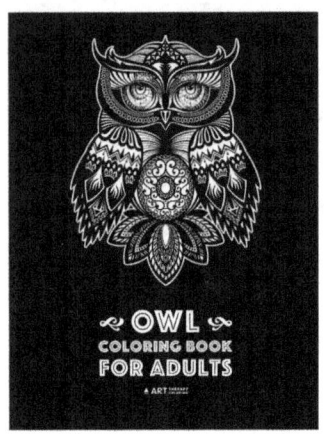

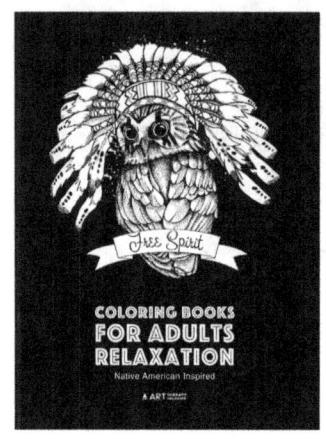

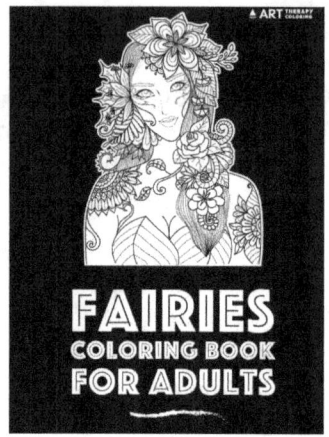

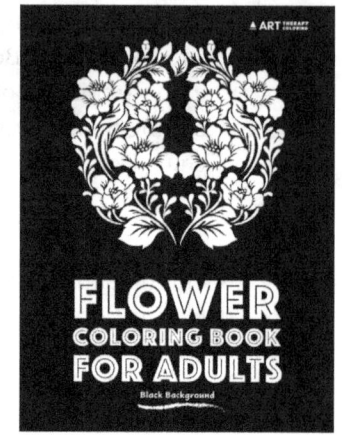

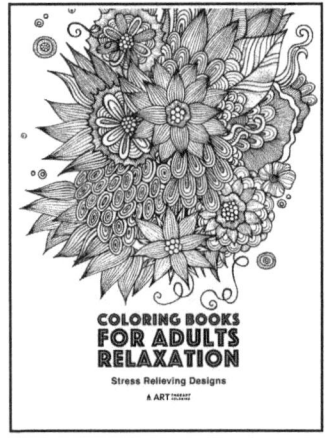

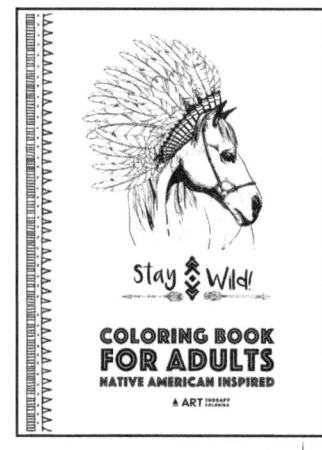

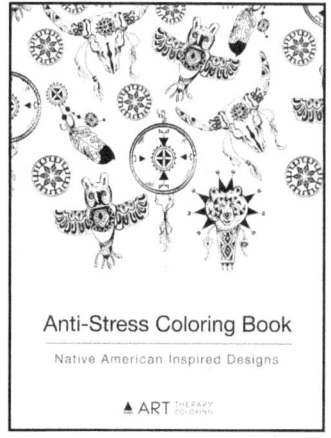

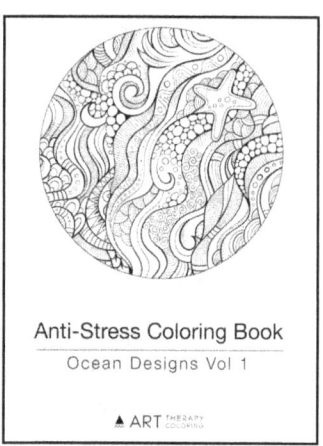

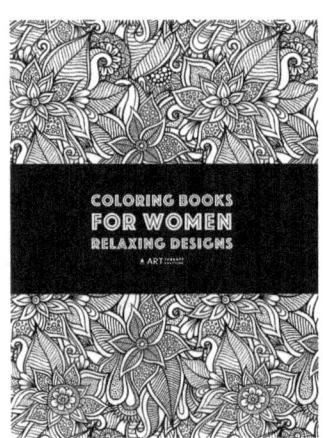

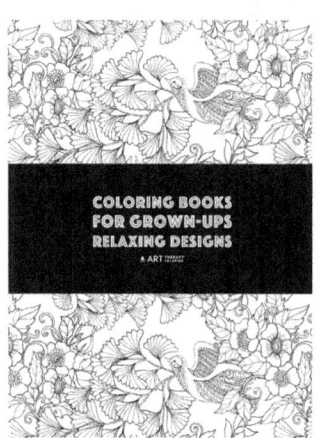

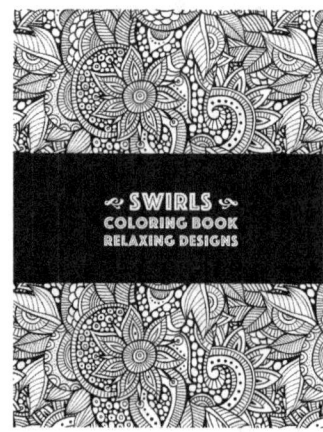

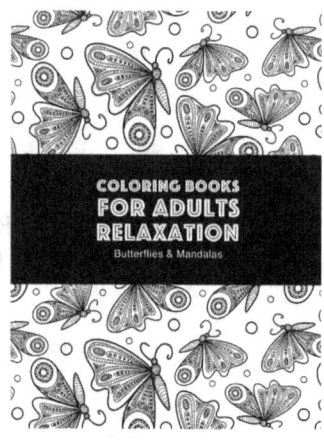

Art Therapy Coloring Books

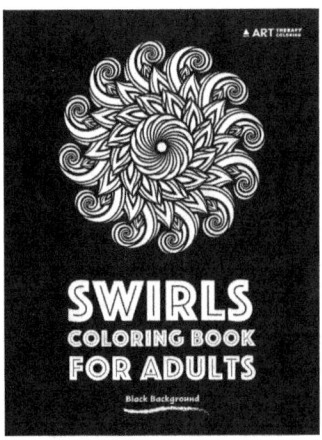

SWIRLS
COLORING BOOK
FOR ADULTS
Black Background

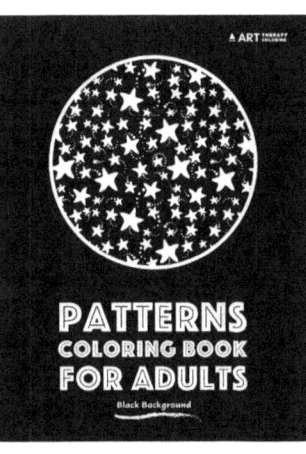

PATTERNS
COLORING BOOK
FOR ADULTS
Black Background

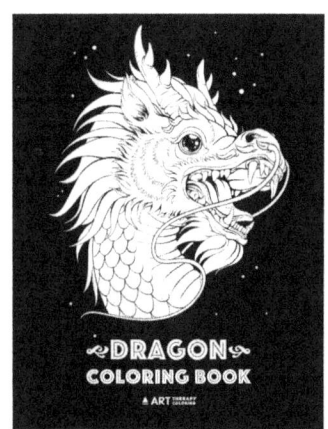

~DRAGON~
COLORING BOOK

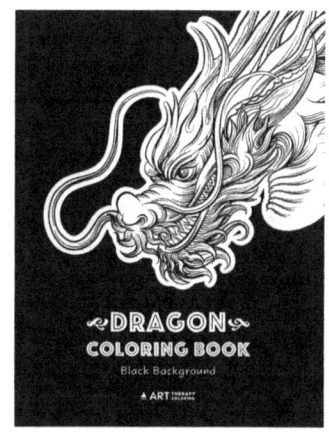

~DRAGON~
COLORING BOOK
Black Background

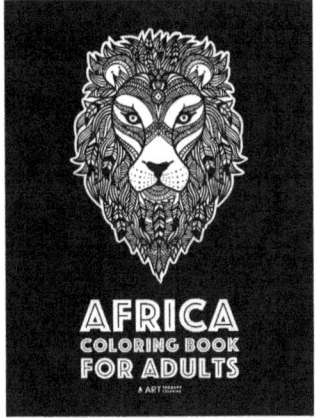

AFRICA
COLORING BOOK
FOR ADULTS

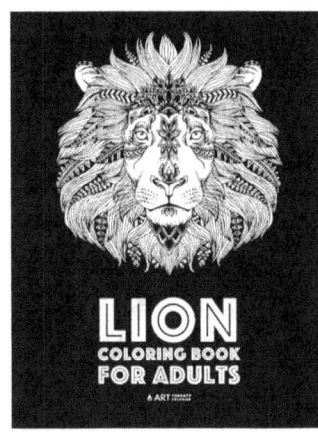

LION
COLORING BOOK
FOR ADULTS

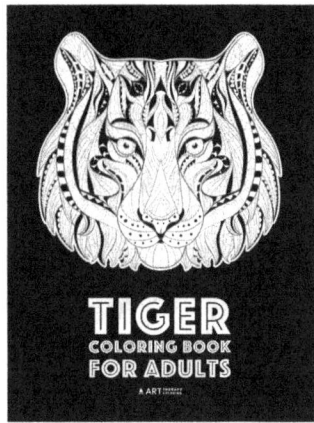

TIGER
COLORING BOOK
FOR ADULTS

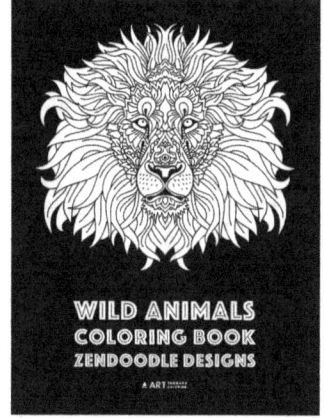

WILD ANIMALS
COLORING BOOK
ZENDOODLE DESIGNS

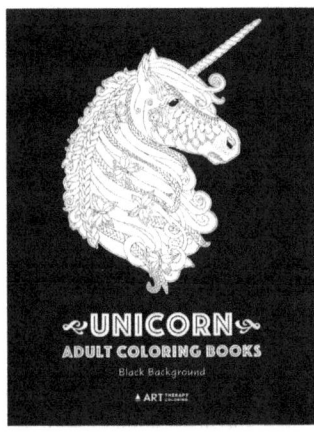

~UNICORN~
ADULT COLORING BOOKS
Black Background

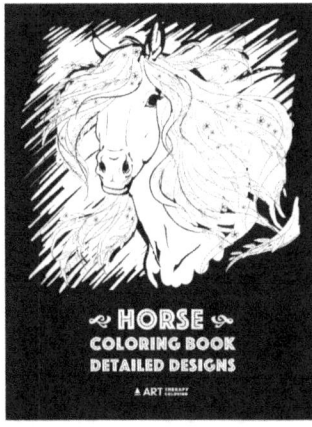

~HORSE~
COLORING BOOK
DETAILED DESIGNS

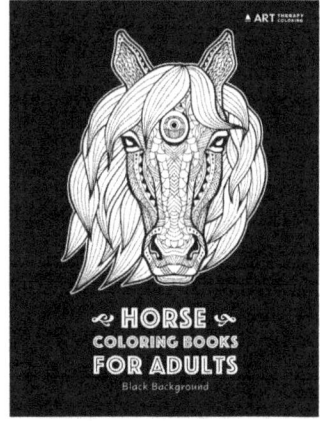

~HORSE~
COLORING BOOKS
FOR ADULTS
Black Background

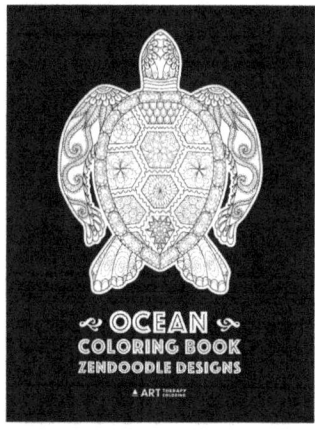

~OCEAN~
COLORING BOOK
ZENDOODLE DESIGNS

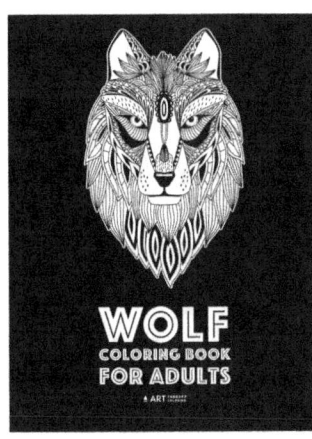

WOLF
COLORING BOOK
FOR ADULTS

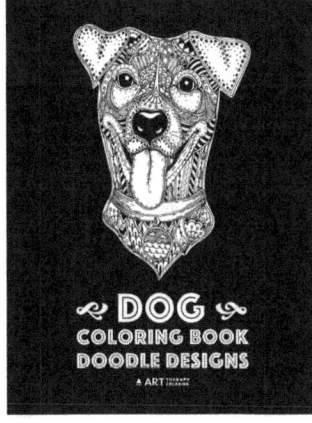

~DOG~
COLORING BOOK
DOODLE DESIGNS

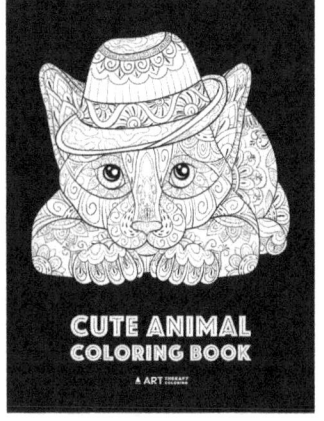

CUTE ANIMAL
COLORING BOOK

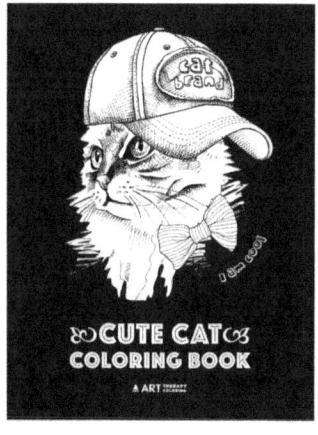

~CUTE CAT~
COLORING BOOK

Art Therapy Coloring Books

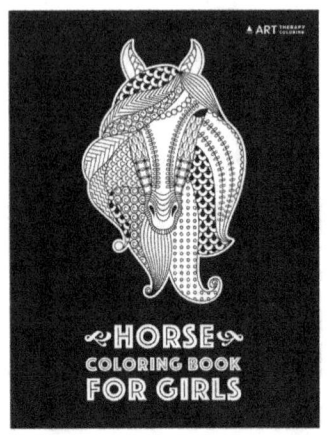

HORSE COLORING BOOK **FOR GIRLS**

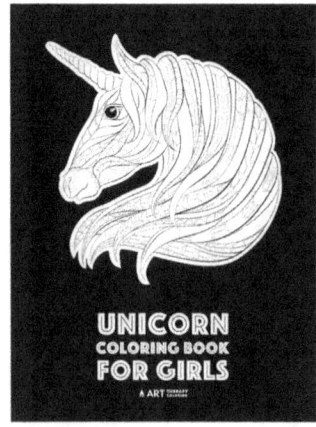

UNICORN COLORING BOOK **FOR GIRLS**

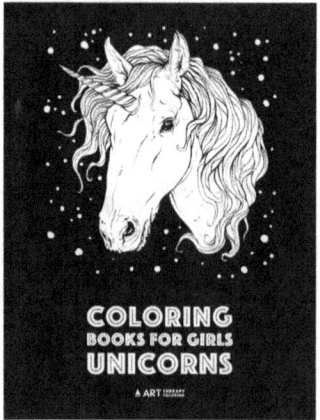

COLORING BOOKS FOR GIRLS **UNICORNS**

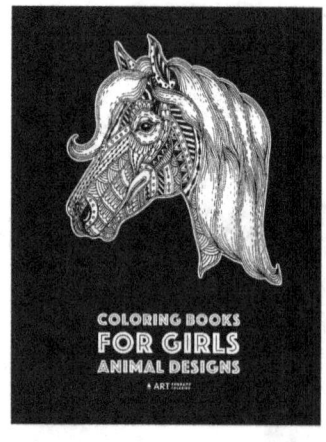

COLORING BOOKS **FOR GIRLS** ANIMAL DESIGNS

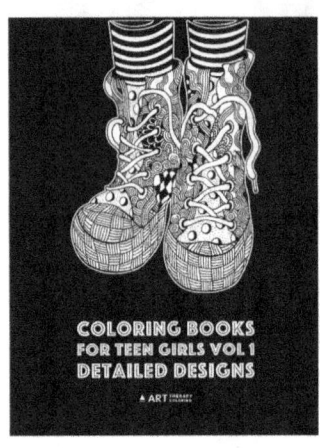

COLORING BOOKS FOR TEEN GIRLS VOL 1 DETAILED DESIGNS

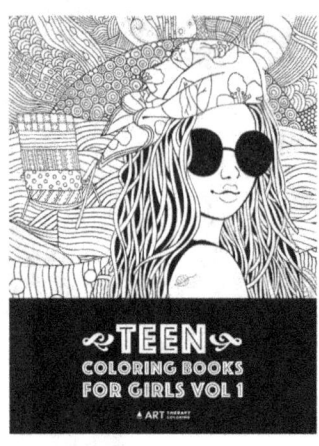

TEEN COLORING BOOKS FOR GIRLS VOL 1

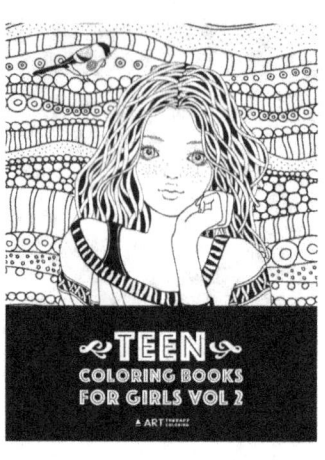

TEEN COLORING BOOKS FOR GIRLS VOL 2

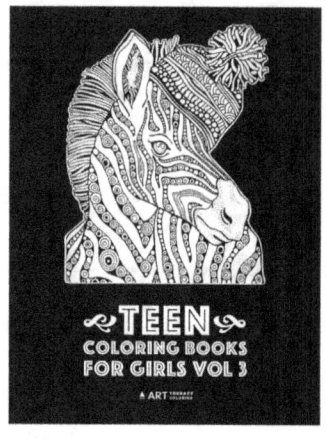

TEEN COLORING BOOKS FOR GIRLS VOL 3

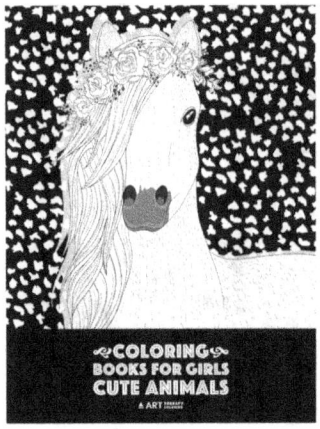

COLORING BOOKS FOR GIRLS **CUTE ANIMALS**

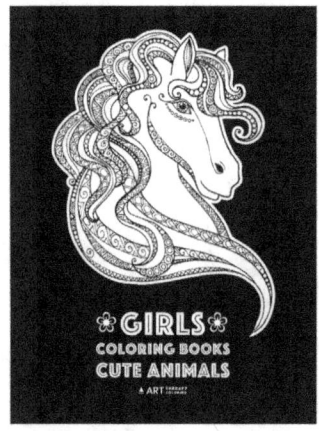

GIRLS COLORING BOOKS **CUTE ANIMALS**

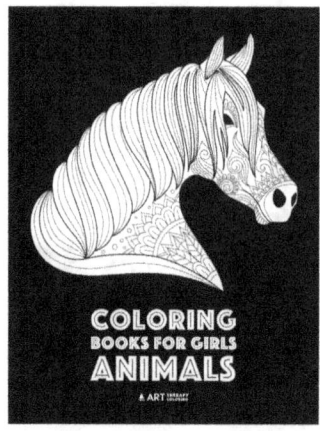

COLORING BOOKS FOR GIRLS **ANIMALS**

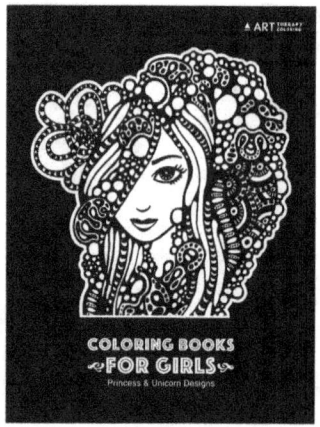

COLORING BOOKS **FOR GIRLS** Princess & Unicorn Designs

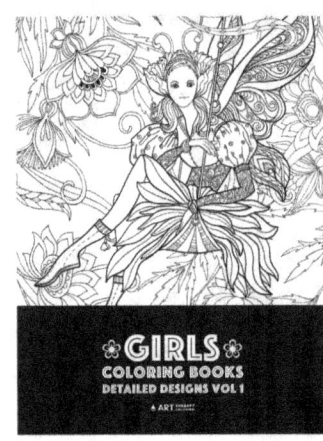

GIRLS COLORING BOOKS DETAILED DESIGNS VOL 1

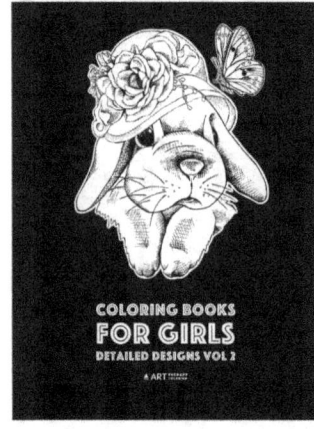

COLORING BOOKS **FOR GIRLS** DETAILED DESIGNS VOL 2

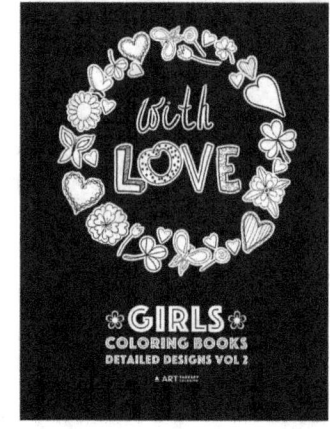

GIRLS COLORING BOOKS DETAILED DESIGNS VOL 2

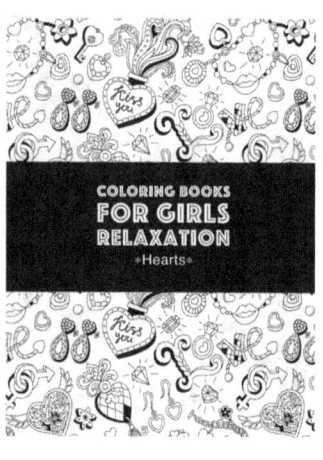

COLORING BOOKS **FOR GIRLS** RELAXATION Hearts

Art Therapy Coloring Books

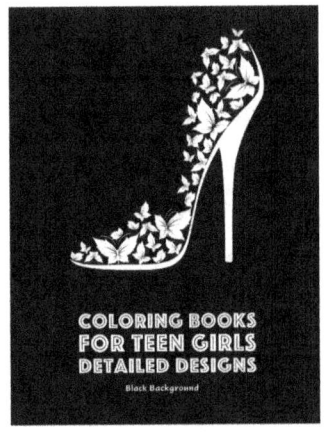

COLORING BOOKS
FOR TEEN GIRLS
DETAILED DESIGNS
Black Background

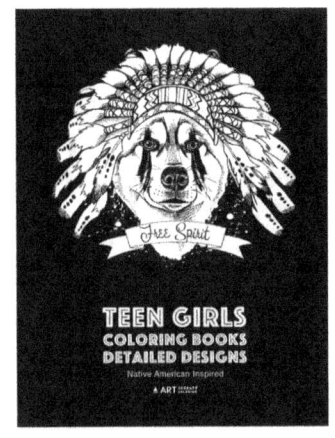

TEEN GIRLS
COLORING BOOKS
DETAILED DESIGNS
Native American Inspired

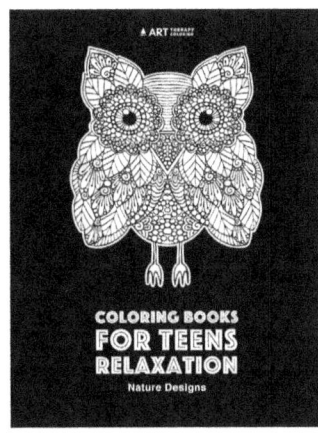

COLORING BOOKS
FOR TEENS
RELAXATION
Nature Designs

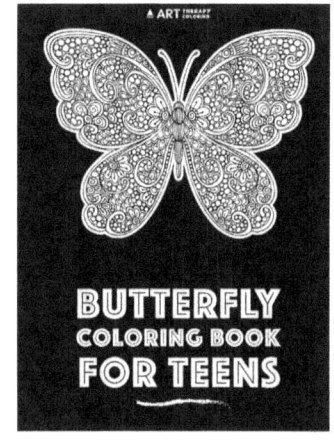

BUTTERFLY
COLORING BOOK
FOR TEENS

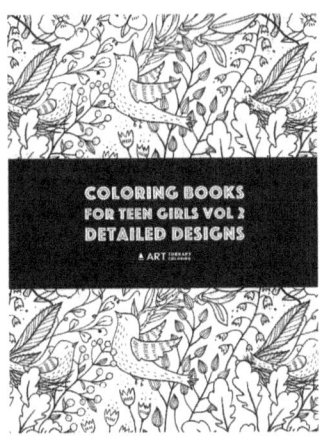

COLORING BOOKS
FOR TEEN GIRLS VOL 2
DETAILED DESIGNS

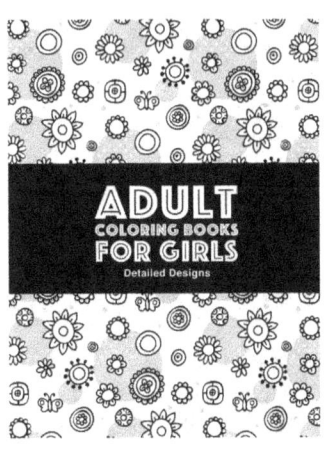

ADULT
COLORING BOOKS
FOR GIRLS
Detailed Designs

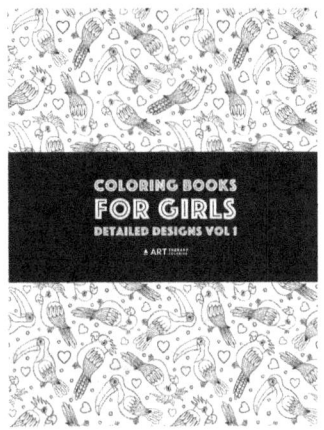

COLORING BOOKS
FOR GIRLS
DETAILED DESIGNS VOL 1

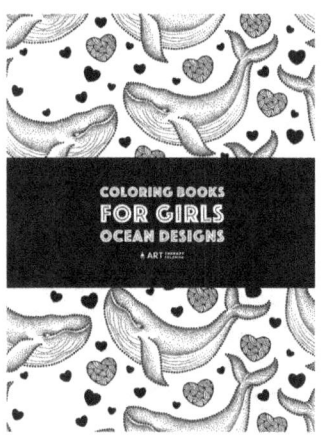

COLORING BOOKS
FOR GIRLS
OCEAN DESIGNS

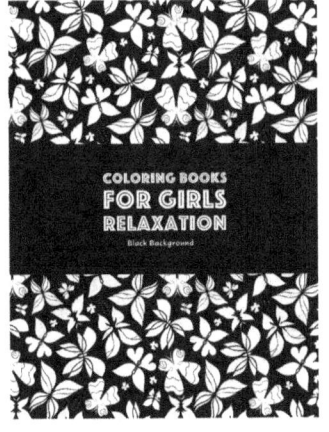

COLORING BOOKS
FOR GIRLS
RELAXATION
Black Background

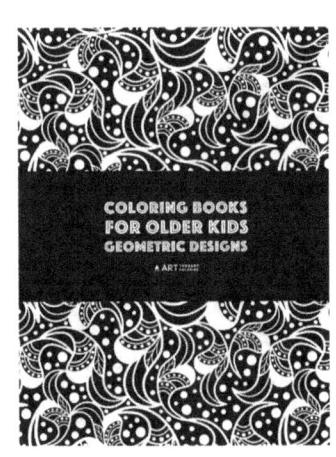

COLORING BOOKS
FOR OLDER KIDS
GEOMETRIC DESIGNS

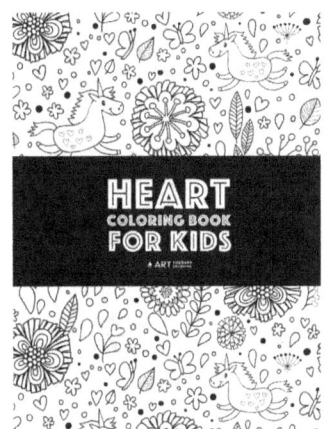

HEART
COLORING BOOK
FOR KIDS

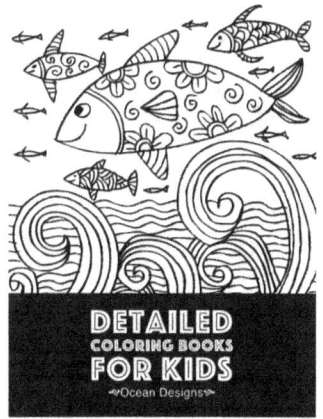

DETAILED
COLORING BOOKS
FOR KIDS
Ocean Designs

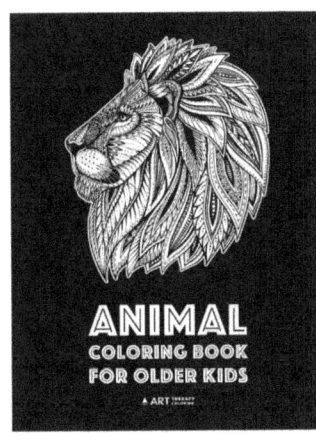

ANIMAL
COLORING BOOK
FOR OLDER KIDS

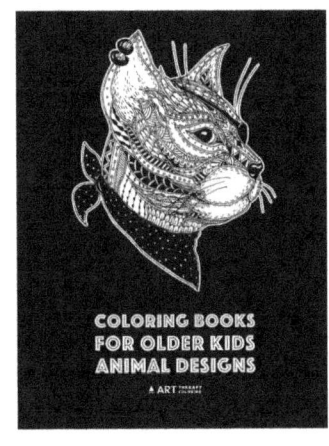

COLORING BOOKS
FOR OLDER KIDS
ANIMAL DESIGNS

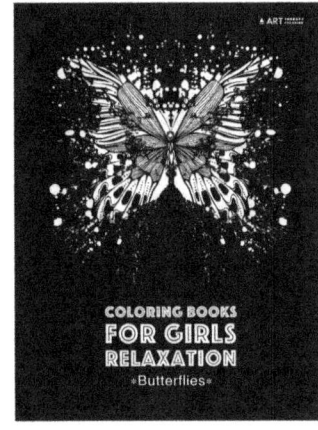

COLORING BOOKS
FOR GIRLS
RELAXATION
Butterflies

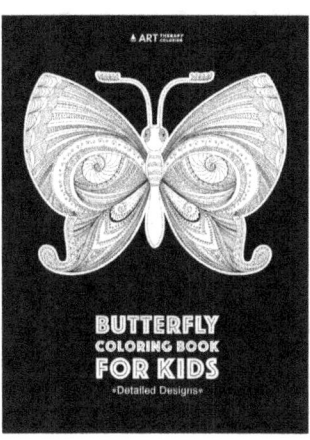

BUTTERFLY
COLORING BOOK
FOR KIDS
Detailed Designs

Art Therapy Coloring Books

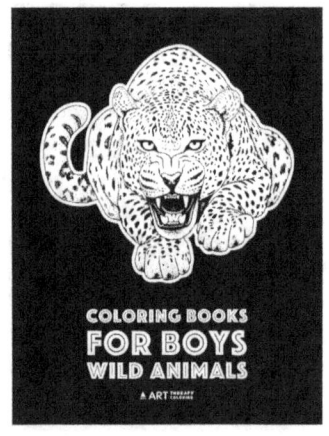

COLORING BOOKS
FOR BOYS
WILD ANIMALS
ART THERAPY COLORING

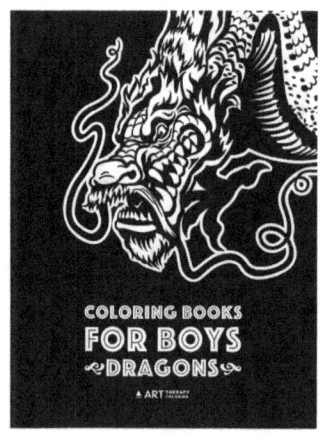

COLORING BOOKS
FOR BOYS
DRAGONS
ART THERAPY COLORING

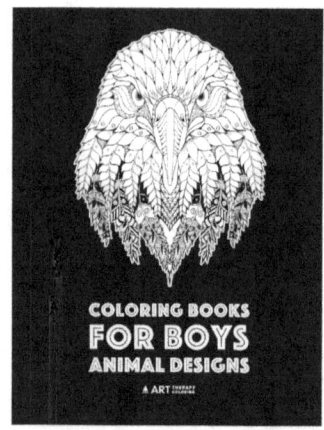

COLORING BOOKS
FOR BOYS
ANIMAL DESIGNS
ART THERAPY COLORING

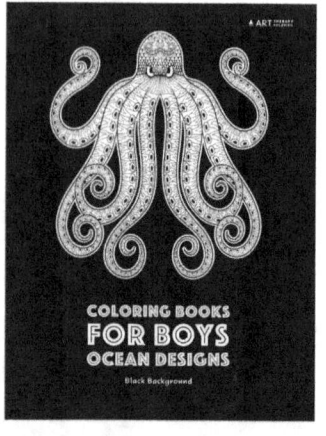

COLORING BOOKS
FOR BOYS
OCEAN DESIGNS
Black Background

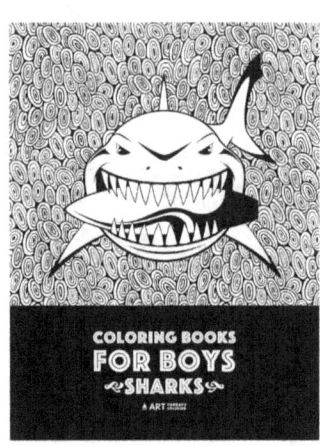

COLORING BOOKS
FOR BOYS
SHARKS
ART THERAPY COLORING

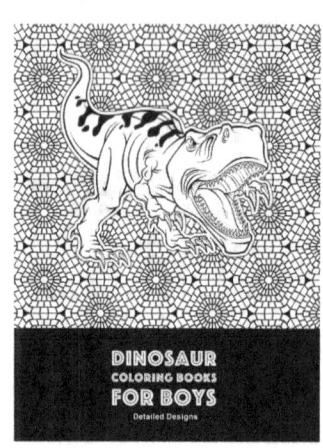

DINOSAUR
COLORING BOOKS
FOR BOYS
Detailed Designs

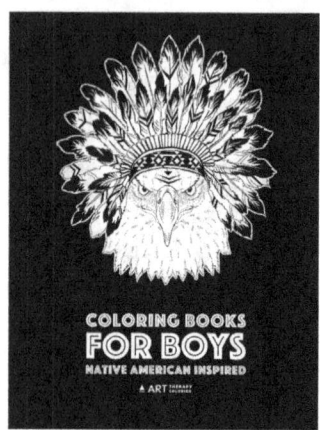

COLORING BOOKS
FOR BOYS
NATIVE AMERICAN INSPIRED
ART THERAPY COLORING

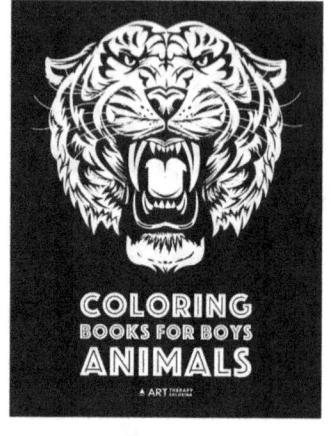

COLORING
BOOKS FOR BOYS
ANIMALS
ART THERAPY COLORING

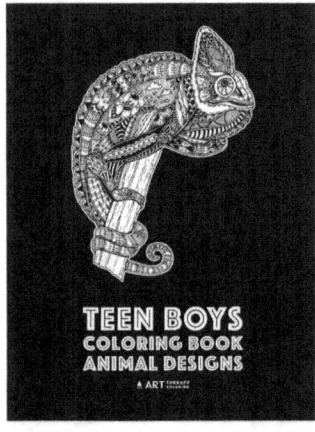

TEEN BOYS
COLORING BOOK
ANIMAL DESIGNS
ART THERAPY COLORING

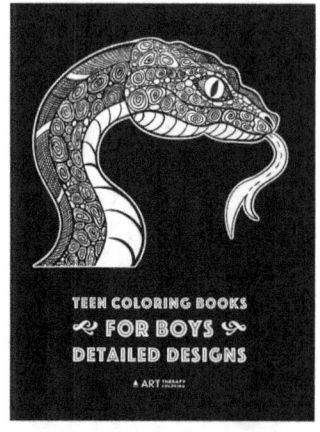

TEEN COLORING BOOKS
FOR BOYS
DETAILED DESIGNS

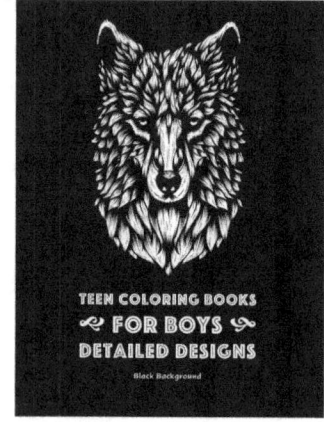

TEEN COLORING BOOKS
FOR BOYS
DETAILED DESIGNS
Black Background

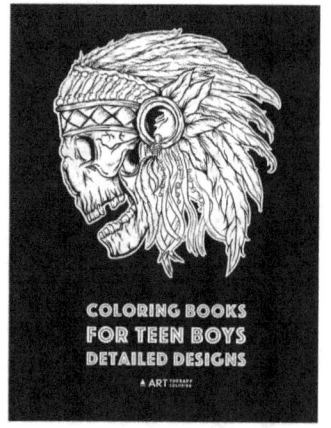

COLORING BOOKS
FOR TEEN BOYS
DETAILED DESIGNS
ART THERAPY COLORING

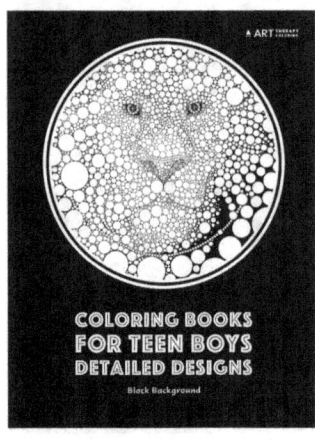

COLORING BOOKS
FOR TEEN BOYS
DETAILED DESIGNS
Black Background

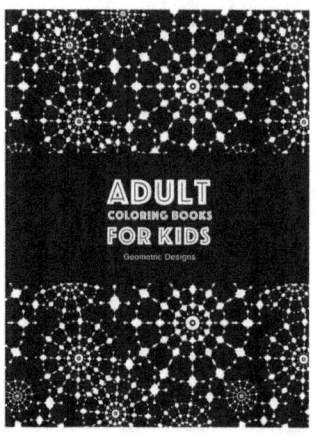

ADULT
COLORING BOOKS
FOR KIDS
Geometric Designs

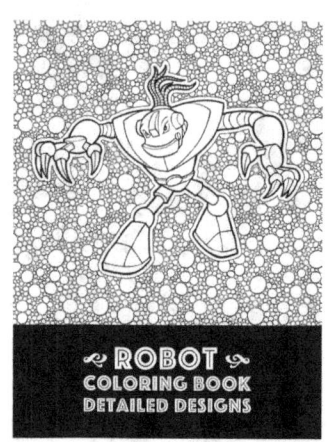

ROBOT
COLORING BOOK
DETAILED DESIGNS

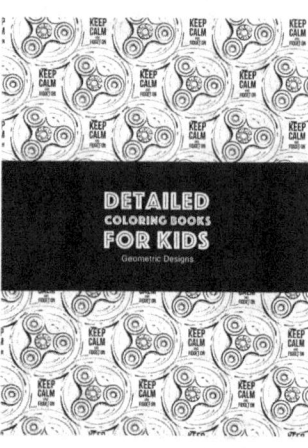

DETAILED
COLORING BOOKS
FOR KIDS
Geometric Designs

Art Therapy Coloring Books

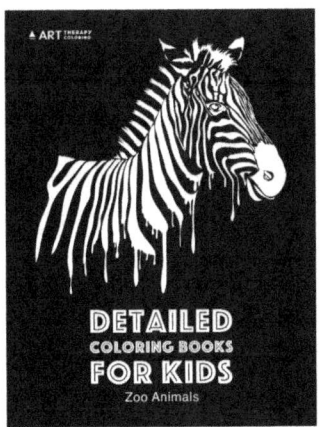

DETAILED COLORING BOOKS FOR KIDS
Zoo Animals

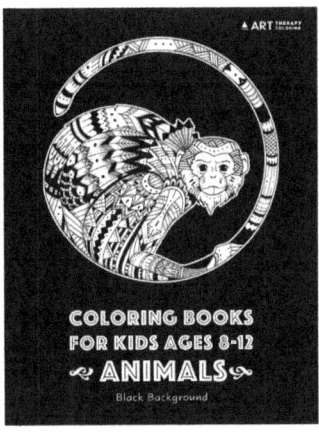

COLORING BOOKS FOR KIDS AGES 8-12 ANIMALS
Black Background

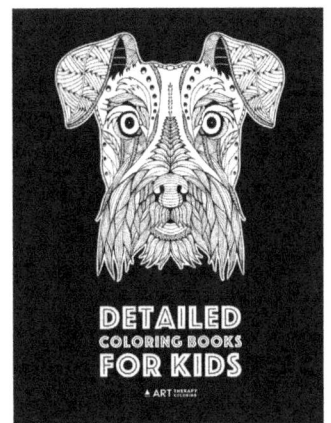

DETAILED COLORING BOOKS FOR KIDS

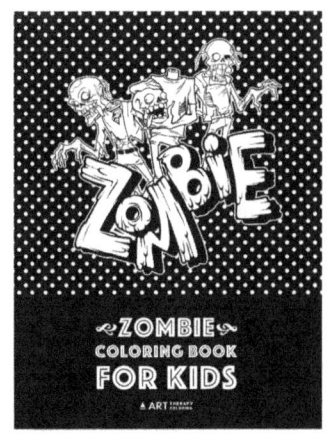

ZOMBIE COLORING BOOK FOR KIDS

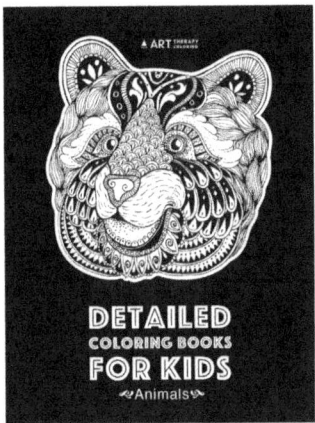

DETAILED COLORING BOOKS FOR KIDS
Animals

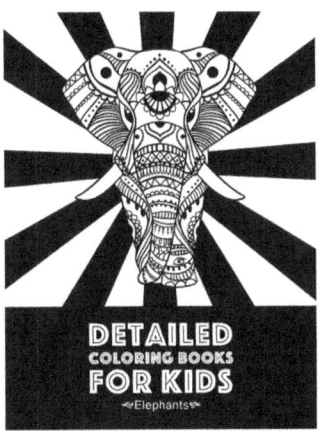

DETAILED COLORING BOOKS FOR KIDS
Elephants

COLORING BOOKS FOR KIDS OCEAN DESIGNS

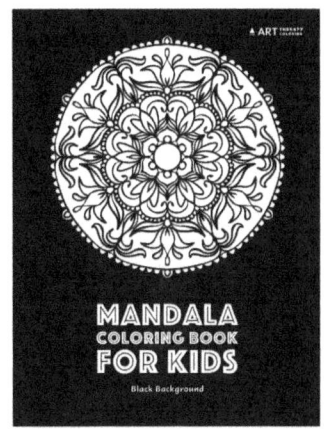

MANDALA COLORING BOOK FOR KIDS
Black Background

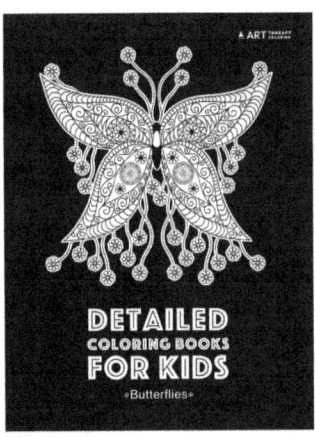

DETAILED COLORING BOOKS FOR KIDS
Butterflies

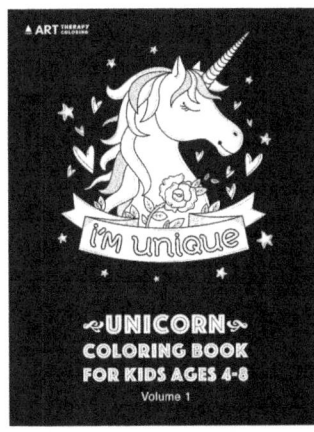

UNICORN COLORING BOOK FOR KIDS AGES 4-8
Volume 1

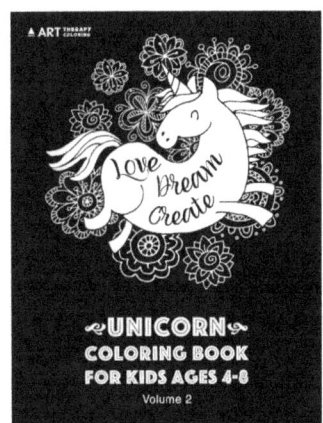

UNICORN COLORING BOOK FOR KIDS AGES 4-8
Volume 2

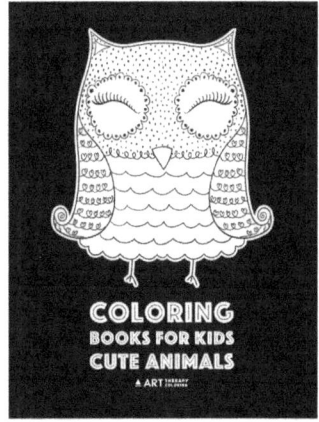

COLORING BOOKS FOR KIDS CUTE ANIMALS

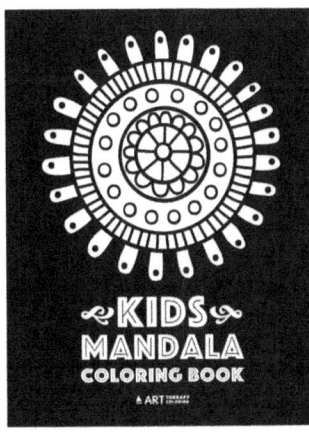

KIDS MANDALA COLORING BOOK

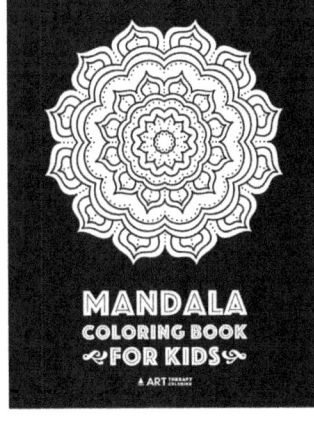

MANDALA COLORING BOOK FOR KIDS

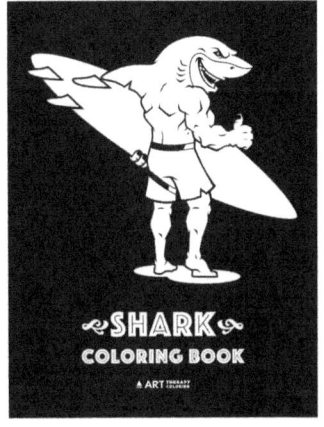

SHARK COLORING BOOK

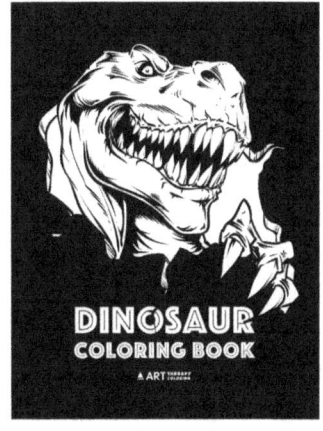

DINOSAUR COLORING BOOK

Coloring Book For Adults
Native American Inspired

Published by:
Art Therapy Coloring
www.arttherapycoloring.com

Copyright © 2017 by Art Therapy Coloring
All Rights Reserved

Shutterstock Images

ISBN: 978-1-64126-004-6

www.ingramcontent.com/pod-product-compliance
Lightning Source LLC
Chambersburg PA
CBHW081343180526
45171CB00006B/589